RUNE
DIVINATION
for today's woman

RUNE
DIVINATION
for today's woman

by

Cassandra Eason

foulsham
London • New York • Toronto • Sydney

foulsham

Bennetts Close, Cippenham, Berkshire SL1 5AP

ISBN 0-572-01813-4

Copyright © 1994 Cassandra Eason.

Phototypeset in by Typesetting Solutions, Slough, Berkshire.
Printed in Great Britain by Cox & Wyman Ltd, Reading.

CONTENTS

What are the Runes?

7

Making and Reading the Runes

15

The Runes

129

Charts

137

WHAT ARE THE RUNES?

At first sight runes look like a child's scrawl on stones or chunks of wood. But in Viking times – and possibly even earlier – people used these strange signs for communication: reading and writing. But even more importantly they used them for making magic – casting the runes. Each sign, they thought, not only had a sound, like A or B, but also had magical properties.

So what has a system that was in use before even your great-grandmother was born got to do with you pushing a trolley round the supermarket with three screaming kids in tow? Or dashing from a business meeting to clean up your flat and cook a three-course dinner because *his* mother's in town and wants to look you over? Well you won't need to use the runes to communicate (unless you fancy putting the fear of God in the boss next time he sends you a nasty memo). But with a little practice you can still tune into the old magic. Not the magic of a load of bloodthirsty male gods waving axes who've never changed a nappy in their lives, but your own very personal magic that you've probably forgotten you've got or never developed because you were so busy taking metalwork classes and trying to fight the boys for the computers. Then you found out that equality was all right in theory, but nobody told you about the impenetrable ceiling that halted the rise of businesswomen, or that men moved the goalposts every time you looked likely to score a winner.

The system is very easy to learn. It takes six weeks and very little pain, because this book with its step-by-step guide is designed to be fitted in to those few odd seconds that you call your spare time. As a working mother of five children, I know how difficult it is to find the time to collapse in front of a soap opera for 10 minutes let alone spend days in meditation. And at whatever stage of life women find themselves, time to do what *they* want is almost always just beyond an ever receding horizon.

The Norse god Odin, the All-Knowing One, learned the secrets of the runes (so legend says) by hanging upside down from the tree of knowledge for nine days and nights. We haven't got that amount of spare time. Instead we need to be like Mrs Odin who was keeping the home fires burning in Valhalla and picking up what she could about the runes while serving up endless banquets for the gods and warriors.

My own introduction to the runes was an absolute let-down. At a psychic fair I had a reading from Mystic Mornay, a very expensive and mysterious looking clairvoyant. She didn't know the names of the runes she used – one did it all psychically she said, as shocked by my question as if I'd asked the colour of her knickers. She treated the runes as psychic dominoes, shuffling them into pairs and making profound but totally irrelevant comments about a golden future, that, given the state of my bank balance and my five children, seemed unlikely – handsome princes with bags of gold and a box of tissues for the kids' runny noses are in short supply where I live.

'Well,' she snapped, eventually losing her psychic cool, 'if you can do any better, I suggest you take it up. Fifteen pounds, please – I don't take cheques.' My next port of call was Wizard Wal of Wolverhampton's stall where I was sold a set of runes at the highly exorbitant price of £15.95. They looked like a set of grey pebbles marked with black felt tip pen and covered with varnish. But then they were magic I was assured. 'No,' said Wizard Wal, 'If you lose one, you can't replace it. Ruins the magic. You have to buy a new set, but I can send them through the post, no extra charge!'

Then there were the books to unravel the key of the stones. Some involved learning 354 different meanings according to whether there was an R in the month and you liked your fish fingers with ketchup. Others involved reading out a page or more of Christmas-card wisdom that bore no relevance whatsoever to the lives of the majority of women: not to the housewife struggling with kids, unresponsive husband and boring part-time job, the older woman trying to cope with elderly relatives, a partner with a prostate and a case of late mid-life crisis nor to someone who has just flown the nest and is trying to keep flat, career and relationships together. Mrs Mythical of the conventional rune books certainly doesn't travel on my train to work.

The clever books were the worst, full of legends of gods and goddesses doing each other down while a dragon nibbled away at the roots of the world tree which a manic squirrel dashed up and down hurling insults at every one. Fascinating stuff, but not much use when the old man throws a wobbly or your statistics are not so vital any more and your jeans have shrunk three sizes in the wash.

I learned there were 24 Norse runes, 29 Anglo-Saxon ones, plus a blank, and even a Celtic set, though the Celts didn't actually use them. Often the experts would admit, after approximately 72 pages, that they didn't know the real meanings or pronunciations. The gaps were, therefore, filled by 'inspiration'.

Wizard Wal's stall had moved on by the time I'd lost my first rune, and I discovered that when all was said and done they were only a set of grey pebbles marked in felt tip. A refund was out of the question.

Besides, I had grown very fond of my grey pebbles, and once I had acquired another one from the beach and had felt-tipped in the missing rune I was back in business with no apparent loss of magic.

Strangest of all, once the window dressing was abandoned and concepts (such as charging herds of bison) had been modified to fit in with the hassle of driving a Lada down the M25 in the rush hour, the stones seemed to work on friends and strangers alike.

Despite their antiquity, runes were relevant. They were a way for ordinary women like myself to look at and take charge of their own lives. I stopped doing readings for men after the stones had turned up a nasty case of marital meanderings. I'd learned enough from all this reading and my knowledge of psychology (an OU Honours degree I'd done while swishing the dish mop round the sink and riding the double buggy across the plains, *and* a large dose of commonsense) to realise that these pebbles, or indeed any pebbles marked in felt tip, were the key to making my own fortune. Mystic Mornay's handsome prince had obviously gone to the wrong house.

On a day trip to the Isle of Wight, where I eventually went to live, I found 30 white pebbles on the beach, bought a 10p piece of felt from the local drapers to use as a casting cloth (to throw the runes on) and a black marker pen.

I was now ready to set up in competition with Mornay. And given the fact she was driving a large shiny car while my Lada sounded like a lawn-mower on its last legs, it seemed no bad idea. But there was the ingredient I hadn't known about, the bit of myself that used to get excited at Christmas and pantomimes. Call it magic, or the intuition that makes a woman suddenly ring up another she hasn't seen for a while and say, 'What's wrong?' All women have this sixth sense, as do children and animals. Men do, too, but it is at odds with the logical image we still push on them.

I worked mainly with women because my world is made up of other women who, like myself, juggle family and job or who try to find a new identity once the kids have flown the nest and are faced, not with freedom, but with dependence by their parents. Hardest of all is the lot of my friends' daughters (the sons seem all to be down the pub or at the match) who have all the problems I faced in my early twenties plus all the expectations the modern world loads on them: that they must be as successful as men, as caring as their mothers and develop their spiritual awareness in the two minutes left. It's no surprise, then, at the end of the day they all wonder what is left of themselves. All dream of that golden tomorrow that just gets further and further away.

I have devised a system whereby women can use the runes for themselves and go on to make their own fortunes, maybe not the ones they dreamed of, but real achievements based on their often forgotten or undeveloped strengths and talents, and within the limitations that their responsibilities have defined. Women don't need clairvoyants (not at the prices some of them charge). Nor do they need me playing Mysterious Mornay, either prophesying their future or deluding them with promises of things that will never turn up in a thousand years.

It's a pity really. I'd invested in dangling earrings and glittery curtain material and imagined myself in a striped booth dispensing wisdom in hushed tones (minus my Midland accent).

All you need to read the runes in six weeks (give or take the odd day for total domestic disasters or downturns of the heart) is this book, a set of pebbles or pieces of wood (perhaps you can persuade number one son or macho brother to expend some of his aggression in sawing an old broom handle into 30 small pieces), a piece of cloth and a waterproof felt tip pen.

Then you are all set to take charge of your own fortune, be your own runic psychotherapist, and your own best friend. You can be the clairvoyant with a guaranteed success rate because you can go out and make the future you predict for yourself.

You don't need my magic – you've got your own. By the second time I gave them a reading women would be saying: 'That stone's linked with the one over there so that means . . . so the best thing I can do is . . . '

'Fine,' I said, taking off my dangling earrings and curtain material, and going to make the tea.

So I'm writing this book before the women I know get too clever and write it first. Eat your heart out Mystic Mornay – the DIY runes' readers are on your trail. Why not buy this book yourself, come out of your tent and get it right?

MAKING AND READING THE RUNES

MAKING AND READING THE RUNES

You need 30 flat pebbles about the size of a 2p piece. One side will be marked and the other left blank so each will need to have a reasonable surface on which to draw, either with a felt tip, marker pen or correcting fluid. Have a day out by the sea or, if not, a couple of hours at the local chalk pit or park will do, anywhere with space around you and a good supply of pebbles.

Day 1

Finding your runes

The magic lies in going by yourself, no kids, no partners, and no mum who'll nag you about wearing a coat and reminisce because 'you were always an odd child'. No, go alone, as this is the first stage in making your own personal fortune as opposed to handing your destiny over to other people to foretell or decide it for you.

You are collecting *yourself* in these stones, the real bits that can be reflected as in a mirror when you cast (the elevated word for throwing) your stones. Children whining for ice creams, elderly relatives demanding a nice cup of tea or boyfriends looking for the nearest pub are definitely not good for your inner harmony. The good mother, daughter, wife, faithful girlfriend or supportive pal is having a day off. Many women only ever go out with other people and end up with a headache because they've been so concerned that everyone else should have a good time.

By selecting what are to become your own runes, not a set made by someone else for you, you are forming them. Already your 30 pebbles are very special. In collecting them you have said, I exist, and I exist apart from other people, much as I love them.

In our society being alone equals being rejected and we fill our lives with people and noise to shut out this fear. We put on the lights because we are afraid of the dark; we invite people we don't like much round after work because our flatmate is away. But in doing so, we lose touch with an important part of ourselves, the special part that makes us uniquely what we are. This magic part has been called intuition, gut feeling, the inner voice and many other names by many so-called experts from philosophers to physicists, but whatever they have called it they have never really captured it. Solitude and listening to the voice deep inside and accepting what you are, not what others would like you to be, will be keys to unlocking the magic. It is a magic that doesn't exist in the sky to be brought down by people who claim to have special access, but the magic bubbling away inside that you knew so well as a child.

If you are by the sea today then walk on the beach and write your name in the sand as you did when you were a child. Only your name – no one else's. Now outline it with your runes before putting them away. You are not conjuring up dark powers but defining your place in the scheme of things. If you are in a park at least mark your initials in runes on a flat area of grass. Do it subtly. A full incantation is likely to bring you before the local magistrates and is not really necessary.

Can you feel the old magic stirring? This is *your* equivalent of sitting on a mountain and meditating, or walking through fields of flowers communing with nature.

Knowing your luck, you will end up fighting off the vandals at the local rec who think that the idea of this lone woman picking up stones and muttering to herself is hilarious. But this is your day. Finish up at an olde worlde teashop or at least the bistro in your local uppercrust department store. Today is no day for Macdonald's or a crowded wine bar.

This need not be a special day. All that has to be done can be sandwiched between a bit of shopping, work, housework, going to classes, collecting kids, sorting out the jumble for the church bazaar and meeting a friend for a moan: whatever passes for an ordinary run-of-the-mill day. Your magic is magic on the run. But it is another step, the outward signs of the stirrings inside. First of all you need something to keep your runes safe and private so they won't get lost or scattered by the kids or buried under a pile of bills. Too often women lose the things that are precious to them, even their moments of privacy.

Being brought up to consider other people's feelings, we say it doesn't matter. But these stones do matter, not because they have to be kept in the dark and untouched because of an out-of-date magic ritual, but because they now stand for a bit of you. From now on you exist, as a separate being with parts that aren't to be trodden on by others. Your rune container is your 'Keep off the grass sign'.

Find, make or buy a box or a drawstring bag (a bag is best). It doesn't have to be expensive but make it something you really like – gaudy, flowery or glittery – to stand for the real you. OK, you might look like Doris Day on steroids if you decked yourself out in pink gingham, but a checked rune bag reminds you every time you see it of the pioneer girl you'd like to be riding bareback over the prairie.

You also need a piece of material about 12 ins square of any colour so long as you can see the runes clearly as they fall on it.

This is to be your casting cloth, but today, like everything else, it is new, unformed and unmarked. Remember when you had something new as a child? It was special to be handled, looked at, marvelled over. Many adults join in the consumer rush trying to recreate that old excitement. But if they look they will find the magic is in themselves, not in the goods.

The magic is there inside you and the runes can draw it out. You can keep your cloth folded inside the bag or box. You don't want to be scrabbling about in plastic bags when you're being mysterious –it spoils the mood.

You also need an indelible marker that will show up on both rune and cloth. You are collecting yourself today, where you begin and end, putting all the bits together to start charting your destiny. Remember the treasure box you had as a child? It wasn't so daft having somewhere special to hide your secret possessions away. You were saying 'there is a special part of me I don't want to share.' But it got taken over like the rest.

When you get home put your new things away safely – don't talk about what you are doing. It is early days and easy to get discouraged if others mock your new-found interest. It is for you and a part of you. Don't even talk to a friend about it, not yet, the cross-flow will only blur the vision and you may end up concentrating on her needs and she on yours.

Now we have our pebbles – our 'runes-in-waiting' – safely tucked in their bags, let's take a few minutes to contemplate their blank surfaces on which we are going to write our separate futures.

Your runes always have one blank side, but this isn't like the reverse of a playing card. They may all look the same but what the blank means in each case depends on what is hiding on the other side. The blank can tell you as much about yourself as the marked side of the rune. If you know what you are hiding, what your blind spot is in a particular situation, you can find out why you need to hide it from yourself.

Of course knowing and acknowledging your blind spots will not automatically get rid of them. Wizard Wal of Wolverhampton may promise to exorcise all your fears by post (just send an SAE and a cheque for £20) but as we know in our heart of hearts – nothing is that simple.

Often the fears we are hiding are real ones and can't be waved away with a magic wand. But we can peep at some of the bogeymen under the bed – secrecy is the fuel of nightmares – and accept we have to live with a particular enemy within or without. If they won't go away when we shout boo, at least they can't creep up on us in the night anymore.

Repression, Freud would have called the blank side of the rune, but then Freud didn't have the washing to do after work as well as acting Miss Sex-puss in bed for a balding partner who complains about your sagging bits, nor did he work for a firm where IQs are still measured in bust sizes.

When you've made your runes and are using them, if a blank falls face up always turn it over very gently. It can hurt especially if the feeling was pushed into the cupboard in childhood.

Sometimes you'll want to cover it up again if you're not quite ready to face an issue. But the time will come when you are. Be as kind to *yourself* as you are about other people's failings and blind spots.

Over the weeks and months you'll see the blank sides less, but they will never completely disappear.

Later you may want to carve a set of more elaborate runes, perhaps making them in silver or using a chisel on stone. Or you could just saw up a chair leg and brand the runes on the wood with a red hot screwdriver. Pottery runes are also possible, but make sure they are strong enough not to crack when you cast them. You can even make rune cakes – the housewives' answer to fortune cookies – that will transform tea with the vicar's wife.

But for now, close your eyes and pull a pebble at random from your box or bag each night and mark it until you have completed the set.

Draw the symbol on the stone with a felt tip and, if you wish, varnish over it. Before you start drawing remember these are your runes and the symbols are just symbols. They have no powers outside your own, which may surprise you, so don't be afraid or think you are dabbling with dark powers. All you are doing is making your own destiny, using the stones as an aid and if you don't make your fortune others will try to mould it for you.

We are using what is considered to be the Anglo-Saxon system because there are 29 symbols which gives us a greater flexibility than the smaller Norse set. Some people dress up in red trousers and perform elaborate ceremonies when making runes, but then they are trying to use them for divination. We're not.

Besides, we are a bit tight for time. If you make one rune a day, it will give you time to get to know each one. If possible, do something for yourself every day, a small treat or time out so you feel positive towards the rune you have made. If it's a really grotty day and everything feels negative, don't make a rune unless you actually want to. You won't make dark runes even if you do feel depressed or slightly malevolent, but there's no point in working on your future when all you want to do is drum your heels. OK, so the book says, 'runes in six weeks', but you're in charge, not me, not the book nor any rune expert. All I'm saying is the system is simple enough to allow you to get to the root of the runes in six weeks. So feel free to choose your own pace and once you've got half-a-dozen runes, you can make the cloth and start working out your destiny.

At the back of the book is a summary of the basic meaning of each rune. But that is like cutting out a dress to fit the pattern of Ms Mythical and then having to add bits and chop pieces off to make it a proper fit for Ms Real Life. The runes are the same. The meanings will change as you make the runes your own and the important issues of your life also move with the months. But this basic 'pattern' should prove useful while you are getting used to the system.

Don't regard the summary as a cheat sheet. Use it as long as you need to: learning the runes isn't like learning your times tables and some of the symbols are so strange that it is only by using them over and over again and matching them against your pattern that they will become second nature. At the outset the name of the rune won't mean as much as what it represents, so use the rune 'meaning' rather than the name if this is easier until you are more familiar with the names.

Runes are traditionally grouped in sets of eight. But this is quite a daunting number to take in all at once. When we start casting the runes we will first do it in sets of three, so it would be more sensible to learn them in threes. We will learn one a day, and every three days we will recap on the three we have just learned.

Feoh
The price
rune

Take a good look at this rune. This is *feoh*, the first in the runic alphabet. It's just three straight lines and very easy to copy. If you have a pencil and a piece of paper handy, try it out. Start with a downstroke then two diagonals off to the right. It's as easy as ABC, easier in fact because the runes do not change and each one is a distinctive shape. Practise on paper until you feel confident, then draw the symbol on your pebble. This rune we call *fay-oh*. Since neither Old English nor Old Norse are spoken in polite society today we can be fairly liberal about using middle-of-the-road pronunciations that won't require taking your tongue to Casualty every ten minutes. No one knows for sure how the names were pronounced, though some may claim to have 'inside information' from upstairs.

Feoh, the price rune, is to do with the price we have to pay, whether for maintaining the present situation or changing the ball game. The original meaning, mobile wealth, applied quite well when people drove their herds of cattle before them. But we are talking about what the cost is, not only the cost to ourselves in material terms, though that sometimes has to be considered, but to our peace of mind and freedom of action if we are constantly in a stress situation, perhaps keeping the peace in the family or trying to cope with an unhappy relationship or problematical career. The cost may have shown itself through headaches or insomnia or generally just feeling tired and ratty. Any change will, of course, have its own price, maybe loss of financial security which can matter if you've got kids or are trying to scrape together the deposit for your first flat. Whether you are 18 or 80 you know there is no such thing as a free lunch; older woman especially may have invested not only all their wordly goods and career prospects in a situation, but also so much of themselves that change cannot be achieved without real pain.

There's also the uncertainty and opposition that comes with trying to alter the way things have been since Noah built the ark.

If you get *feoh* as your rune of the day, or in a reading, ten-to-one the price of something in your life has seemed a bit high lately and you have to decide if it is worth carrying on paying.

If *feoh* is hidden, then the price being asked is more than the obvious one. Dig deeper and find what is really being asked of you.

Maybe you are happy to go on paying. Also, in some situations, there is a hidden pay-back that satisfies the need to feel approved of and to be thought indispensable. This pay-back keeps many women in situations that on the surface appear to ask too much and give nothing in return. Only you can ultimately decide if you are paying a price that is acceptable to you, and no-one, clairvoyant or best friend, has the right to make this decision for you. You are making your own destiny. In the runes there are no right answers except those you give.

At the end of the chapter and at the back of the book is a mini-definition for *feoh*.

Ur, the obstacle rune, is to do with the people or situations that block our way forward either at work or home. Originally *ur* referred to the charging herds of bison (or aurochs as they were called in those days when every well-dressed fellow sported a blood-axe and a pair of horns). You can pronounce *ur 'er'* as in *''er indoors'*. Sometimes there are very real obstacles in our path, even if you're not being hassled by a herd of oversized cows.

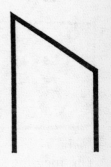

Ur
The obstacle rune

The obstacle can be a person: your mother or the office dragon; even husbands and children can put up incredible obstacles if we try to make improvements in our lives. Grandmothers especially can find that it's not only their partners who are resistant to change but grown-up children, also, who expect Mum to be there for the grandchildren as she was for them. Elderly relatives can block innovation in your life not only with their physical demands, but with emotional blackmail built up over a lifetime.

Sometimes the obstacles are within us like the fear of failing or seeming pushy, which have been built up during all those years when nice girls were expected to stand back and make the jam sandwiches while big brother went out and slew the dragons at the end of the street. The internal obstacles can be the hardest of all to shift. Sometimes we put up obstacles without realising it, because we don't actually want to do things we feel we ought to or are good for us.

When you get *ur* in a reading, there is something blocking your path. You must then ask yourself if this obstacle can be removed or whether you must go round it. Is it an outside force or created by your own fears? If *ur* is hidden, it may be that we keep creating objects in our path because deep down we prefer the *status quo*. If there is something you really don't want to change, then accept it: you are making your own destiny so are perfectly free to take that decision. You don't need to hide behind self-imposed barriers in seeking to justify your way of life to yourself or anyone else.

Day 5

Thorn
The niggling rune

Thorn, the niggling rune, means just that. It even looks like a thorn sticking out of a branch, the type that makes you say 'ouch' if your finger touches one. *Thorn* refers to life's irritations that nag away at your peace of mind and self-confidence rather than the life or death issues that blow your mind. It talks of the little resentments, the petty injustices in family or work life that make you reach for an extra bar of chocolate, a cigarette or another drink.

Women tend not to throw minor annoyances back, but keep the anger inside themselves and let all the little niggling incidents build up.

Then one day the checkout girl in the supermarket will be a bit off-hand or the nosey old girl at the end of the street will make some snide remark about your boyfriend staying three nights in a row and wow! the lid's off, the offending mortal gets it for the lot – from husband's failure to fix the freezer door, for the fortieth time of asking, to the secretary in the office always using your erasing fluid without asking and never putting the top back so it's dried up when you need it. 'What's the matter with her? What did I say?' they cry as you threaten to throw the office computer through the window. Then you end up apologising and feeling an absolute idiot.

Thorn can indicate that these niggling injustices are starting to bug you. Where possible, deal with each irritant as it arises rather than suffer in resentful silence. Explain politely but clearly why you feel aggrieved and suggest an alternative whereby the *thorn* can lose its barb. If you place, rather than throw, the hostile or thoughtless action in the lap of the perpetrator, you'll find you need to smoke or eat less as a reaction and avoid those over-the-top scenes where you end up with egg on your face and the cause of the hassle comes up smelling of roses.

If *thorn* is hidden it may be you are not admitting to yourself that you are being bugged by something or someone because you feel that it is not 'nice' to be annoyed. But we all get annoyed by other people. Plaster saints are best in churches. Anyway, have you noticed all the lines they get from those fixed smiles?

Six days in and the positive vibes are gleaming and glistening like a telly washing-powder ad. But we haven't actually used our magic pebbles, so, let's do a rune of the day reading for someone else. This reading, like others in the book, is based on one that I actually gave to someone.

Mary's cast of three

Mary is in her late forties and an administrator for a charity which involves working with several temperamental men. She answers the phone and deals with the callers, some of whom can be very difficult. Mary is always smiling and helpful. She has a very nice, but demanding, teenage son, who treats the house like a hotel, and a weak and charming husband who fritters away money like a child. Mary is overweight and a heavy smoker and these things distress her. She suffers from frequent stomach upsets and migraines.

Mary's reading

The first rune Mary draws out is ᚦ *thorn*. The second is ᚠ *feoh* but this is hidden. The third is ᚢ *ur*.

What would you tell Mary that her runes suggest? Remember not to offer a solution. That is for her to decide. Use the mini-definitions at the end of this section or read through the chapter again. There are no rights or wrongs so you may give Mary a completely different reading from mine.

I saw Mary's life being made up of many minor hassles *(thorn)*.

She wasn't reacting to them openly but smoking and eating a lot to swallow her anger and getting lots of internal churnings. Mary knows that a lot of people will get very upset if she changes things so the price *(feoh)* of change is quite high. But it is the hidden payback that perhaps is important and keeps Mary in a situation where on the surface the price seems too high. Mary knows she is indispensable to all these people and the sense of approval and of being needed is important to her. The obstacles to any change are great *(ur)*. Only Mary can decide whether she will accept that she is put upon, but that the benefits outweigh the disadvantages, or whether she is no longer prepared to be a doormat. In either case, by acknowledging the situation and accepting it she is choosing what to do, thus her level of tension will be dramatically reduced.

Now sort out the runes you have made and put them in the bag. Take out one and put it down on the table or floor without looking.

Your rune of the day

Whenever you do a reading, only use the marked runes you have made. For now put the unmarked stones aside. The last rune of all will always be left blank but we'll talk about that when the time comes because in a way that is the most important rune of all. Note the rune you chose on the chart at the back of the book, drawing the symbol and indicating whether it is hidden or not. OK, with three runes we're not going to get a representative reading but you can at least start to find out what each rune means for you.

1 Which rune is it?
2 Is it hidden?
3 How does the meaning fit in with what is going on in your life? If it doesn't make a lot of sense by itself, wait till you've charted the next two days and then you'll have more of a picture.

Summary

ᚠ *Feoh (fay-oh)* is the price rune, what you must pay for achieving what you want or for maintaining the *status quo*. If hidden, the price is more than it seems.

ᚢ *Ur (er)* is the obstacle rune which tries to tell you what is blocking your ambitions. If it is hidden, it may be telling you that you need the obstacle and don't want change.

ᚦ *Thorn* is the niggle rune, the one that reveals the many petty annoyances that are building. If it is hidden, then perhaps you feel you have no right to be annoyed with those who are disturbing you.

Day 7

Os (pronounced like *toast* without the two 't's) is to do with communication. It means mouth and this is the part of the body that generally gets people into trouble. *Os* has two sides, listening and speaking. Women are considered good listeners in the sense they will usually let others rabbit on for hours about their problems. But often we don't actually listen to the things that really matter.

We assume we know what those closest to us are saying because we are reacting not to their actual words but to those old scripts we learned way back. The old rejections, the old put-downs run through our minds and we reply with anger remembering the injustices that began to bug us long ago. The other guy, of course, is not necessarily hearing us either, because he's living with old playground disputes that went unresolved. So communication can end up with two sets of ghosts arguing. It is important to start to communicate our immediate needs and to attack the way things are rather than the people who are behaving unfairly to us.

Os

The rune of communication

Equally it is important to listen to what the other person is actually saying and try to find the real message behind yesterday's garbage.

In a reading *os* can mean that communication is an issue in your life at the moment; there is a lot of real talking to be done if you are to go forward and not just let it all go round and round in your head, keeping you awake and building up inner resentments or regrets.

If *os* is hidden, then maybe you aren't actually listening to what is being said, but are just running those old memory tapes through again and again. Perhaps, too, you are not saying what you want or need to say to the person concerned, but talking to the ghost standing behind him.

Now do your second rune of the day reading, using the new rune as well as the first three. See which of the four runes emerges. Was it the same one as yesterday? Is it hidden? What is it saying? Use the mini-definitions at the back of the book to help you. Each day the readings will get clearer.

Day 8

Rad
The rune of the rough ride

Rad looks like a very angular 'R' and that is the sound it signifies. It is pronounced *'rard'* to rhyme with hard and that's what it's about, the kick-in-the-pants rune. *Rad* used to mean ride and as the Old English rune poem caustically observes, it is easier to talk about the journey you want to make than actually getting up and going. Loads of those old warriors would sit around in the comfort of the great hall talking about their past great conquests. But they weren't actually out there doing it.

Don't panic. Getting on with something is much more exciting than sitting at home with the old photos and memories, speculating morosely on how things might have been and then immersing yourself in a TV soap opera. It's no use, either, sitting reading one of those slushy books or magazines where the young heroine meets the wise and rich older guy in an exotic location and lives comfortably ever after. The only older guys you are likely to meet are twice divorced with a heavy maintenance bill for their kids and an impending hernia if they do more than change the channel on the telly. Those exotic locations may be there but it's you who would have to pay the return fare.

Rad in a reading may suggest some change that you have been thinking about making is due. Just take your courage in both hands and make even a small change. For every act of destruction of the old order, even if it's only to stop watching television every night, replace it with something new and positive, something you want to do, a step forward. There's no point in trampling the old underfoot unless you've got a new direction to ride in. This isn't like fortune-telling. The appearance of this rune doesn't mean a great hand is going to swoop down from the sky and take away your familiar world. Changes are caused by people themselves. But it may take a bit of courage to get started.

If *Rad* is hidden, then maybe you're kidding yourself that the safe option is what you want. It's easier to look at the old photos, but why not go out and take some more?

Now do your third rune of the day reading putting the five runes you have made into the bag, choosing one and marking it in the back of your book, next to yesterday's. What are the three runes you have chosen saying? Use your mini-definitions or read back. Take your time and don't worry if there's nothing profound. You are looking at the issues around you and taking charge of your own destiny.

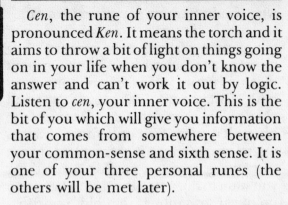

Day 9

Cen
The rune of your inner flame

Cen, the rune of your inner voice, is pronounced *Ken*. It means the torch and it aims to throw a bit of light on things going on in your life when you don't know the answer and can't work it out by logic. Listen to *cen*, your inner voice. This is the bit of you which will give you information that comes from somewhere between your common-sense and sixth sense. It is one of your three personal runes (the others will be met later).

You won't always be pleased to see this rune because sometimes this voice won't flatter you or let you off the hook. You can't kid yourself when *cen* speaks. But its words are pure magic, your magic.

This is the clairvoyant with the 100 per cent success rate because it knows the subject inside out. It does not need to pluck predictions from the sky but can delve deep into those strange parts of you that are buried so deep that you can't even remember them. It is the rune that can refresh parts of you that other runes can't.

In a reading *cen* suggests you do know the answer to most questions if you can only trust this inner judgement in a critical situation. 'What should I do?' I was asked during my brief guru phase with the curtain material and dangly earrings. It was tempting to pretend to pluck the answers out of the sky. But instead I would ask 'If I were you what would you tell me to do in this situation?' Ten minutes later they'd go off having answered their own questions quite easily, and weeks or months later, after they had manipulated their destinies quite unconsciously, things would come to pass according to what their *cen* had advised them.

If *cen* is hidden, you may be afraid to listen to yourself. Trust your own judgement – it will be the first solution that comes to you urgently but without any apparent reason. *Cen* comes from the magic that is within you and nothing is beyond our *cen*!

Now you are beginning your second rune of the day trio. As you make more runes, they will be more representative. But each rune has something to say, so these early readings help you to sort out the basic issues in your life. Take a rune from the bag without looking. You've got six to choose from now, so the runes can start to vie to be heard. Now draw its symbol on the chart at the back and note if it is hidden. How does it add to what your last three runes are saying? Remember, though we are working in threes, the whole lot make a continuing story, your story.

Christine's cast of three

Let's do another rune of the day reading for someone else.

Christine is in her late twenties and has just broken up from her third live-in relationship and is wondering whether to move in with a much older man she has met. In all her relationships she has fallen for men who will take care of her, but then she kicks against the restrictions this puts on her. She ends up having violent rows and walking out, leaving everything behind.

Christine's reading

Christine's first rune is ᚠ *os* which is hidden. Her second is ᚳ *cen* which is also hidden and the third is ᚱ *rad*, again hidden. Christine wonders whether she should embark on this new relationship. What would her reading suggest to you? My interpretation, which is no more likely to be right than yours and certainly nowhere near as accurate as Christine's own assessment of the stones, would see *os* hidden as suggesting that Chris is not really communicating with any of her partners but carrying on a long-standing argument with her own father that might have started in her early adolescence.

Cen is also hidden which implies that Chris really knows the answer to her own question but isn't facing up to the facts about the likelihood of success in entering into another father/daughter scenario without sorting out the issues within herself.

Rad is the clue. It might seem Chris has been having a hard ride, but in fact she has been taking the soft option, handing over responsibility to other people and then complaining when it doesn't work out. There is a need perhaps for a real **change in** Chris herself, maybe a spell on her own getting used to running her own show, before she enters a new relationship. In the end only Chris can say what is best for herself, which she will be able to do once she is aware what is bubbling under the surface. If she chooses to go ahead with the new man, at least she will enter the new relationship with her eyes open.

Now do your rune of the day (you have six runes to choose from now). Draw the symbol on the chart at the back and again see if it is hidden.

What do the new runes suggest? Can you link them with the last three you drew? Are you getting mainly blanks or are things coming into the open? Tomorrow we will start to make the casting cloth now you've got something to throw.

Summary

ṱ   *Os (oas)* is the communication rune. Something important has to be said. If *os* is hidden you may be listening to yesterday's conversation.

Ṙ   *Rad (rard)* is the kick in the pants rune that suggests change is long due which may be hard but promises excitement. If *rad* is hidden, are you taking the soft option, sitting on your butt and complaining you don't like the way things are?

ᚳ *Cen (ken)* is the rune of your inner voice. Listen to it. It is rarely wrong. *Cen* in a reading may mean you have been receiving a lot of conflicting advice. You yourself know what is best. If *cen* is hidden then you are letting other people dictate your destiny. If you do, you can't complain if it goes wrong.

Day 11

Making the casting cloth

This is a big day with a lot to do and remember. But take as long as you like and if you feel you need to stop here and go over this section again in the next few days then do so. After all, there is no Great Runemaster in the sky holding a stopwatch over you.

Find the piece of cloth you bought: get a saucer, a tea plate and a small dinner plate to draw round. Whether you use Crown Derby or reject crockery from the market will not affect the magic. Of course you may be one of those brilliant people who can draw perfect circles freehand — if so I probably pulled your pigtails at school.

In the centre draw round the saucer with a felt tip pen. You have now drawn your circle of *Being*, the Inner You, so anything that falls in this area is going to be connected to the real, deep down person and is therefore pretty important.

At first you may find there's not much rune activity here; you may, like most of us, have become very out of touch with your real self.

Runes that do fall here may first be hidden – women are brought up to deny the powerful emotions that are as much a part of us as the love and caring side. Don't worry about trying to remember all this; it is summarised at the end of the chapter and at the end of the book.

Next we are going to draw your circle of *Thinking* – where your thoughts, hopes, fears and feelings hang out or hide. Place a tea plate over the saucer circle and draw round the edge. You have now created the circle of your mind. This second circle is the place where the inner you gets ready

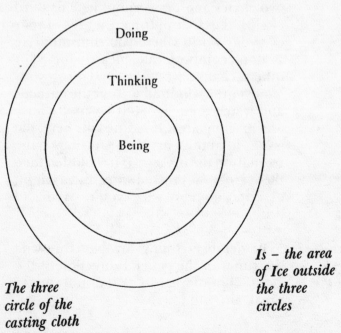

Doing

Thinking

Being

The three circle of the casting cloth

Is – the area of Ice outside the three circles

to spring into action, where you rehearse your conversations, dream your dreams and sometimes plan your battles.

Of course it can still get pretty clogged up with the thoughts and expectations (real and imagined) of other people. If you get hidden runes in this circle it can suggest that most of the action is taking place here in your head and not out in the real world. If, when you start casting, your circle of thoughts is empty maybe you should eavesdrop on your dreams to find out what it is that you can't face thinking about.

Now place a dinner plate over the other two circles and draw round it. This third circle is the circle of *Doing*, the area of your everyday world where you communicate or don't communicate, please yourself or others, change everything and throw your hat over the windmill or shut the curtains and watch the telly. So it's a pretty busy and exciting area. If a rune falls here, the issue it represents is featuring quite strongly in the present. If it is hidden then there are some crossed wires and a fair bit of opposition to what you're trying to do.

The Great Mystery – casting the runes

Remember casting involves throwing the runes in the general direction of the cloth – not too hard – you don't want to break any windows.

It's not a game of hoop-la or darts where the idea is to hit the centre or a passing god. You don't need to dance round the garden gnome twice in your frillies or starve yourself for 24 hours to get the psyche gnawing away.

When you want to do a cast, just sit down in peace with your cloth and the marked runes in the bag. Let the runes go where they want (within reason). This is the bit where psychology and self-awareness get left behind in the rune bag. Which rune falls where and why, who knows? Don't worry about it, just use the information to make this fortune you've been dreaming of. At the same time it's possibly a home help you need galloping to the door rather than a rusty prince who'll only want you to wait on him. Or perhaps you can dispense with princes altogether and get a slice of the action for yourself?

Have a practice session throwing the runes and see where they land. Just get the feel of letting them fall. Don't note anything down yet. Take three runes at a time from the bag and throw them on the cloth.

If a rune falls in the outer circle, the circle of *Doing*, then we know it's to do with the actual events of our life.

If it falls in the middle circle, the circle of *Thinking*, it's what's in our mind, and if it falls in the central circle, the circle of *Being*, then it's something very central in our lives. Is it hidden? Is it close or on top of other runes? If it's on a line, it's a bit of both.

Is
Outside
the circles

But. . . what if your runes don't fall in any of the circles when you throw them? Then they are in the area we call *Is* (pronounced *eess*).

Is is the name of a rune that means ice. It is also the name of the most important area of the rune cloth. Outside the circles is the area of *Is* which includes the table, if you have your cloth on the table, or the floor if you are kneeling on the floor casting your runes (very spiritual if your knees can stand it). If your rune is on *Is* it means exactly that – stuck, frozen, immobile. A hidden rune on ice means nobody's going far without a blowlamp.

Ice is cold, slippery, can be liable to crack unexpectedly, not a brilliant place to be. But sometimes you have to put things on ice till you're ready for them or if circumstances are preventing you making changes. If something is hidden in *Is* then it suggests that you may be limiting yourself by not facing up to an issue.

Now we're going to do a cast of three for somone else to give you an idea how the system works.

Ellie is in her mid-twenties and has worked for the same firm since she left school and has carved out a niche for herself where she is responsible for customer care. However she is bored rigid and finds herself having less patience than she used to with the complaints from the public that are the core of her work. Lately she has spent more and more of her free time working on her animal paintings and has accepted several commissions to paint or draw people's pets. She has seriously been thinking about going freelance, but her parents point out that if she does so she will never be able to afford the deposit on the flat she was contemplating buying but, instead, will have to remain in her cramped bedsit.

Ellie's cast of three

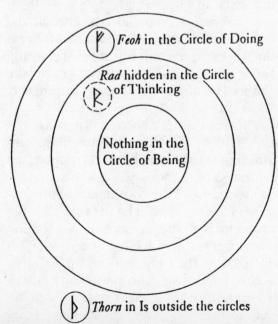

Feoh in the Circle of Doing

Rad hidden in the Circle of Thinking

Nothing in the Circle of Being

Thorn in Is outside the circles

Ellie casts ᚱ *rad* hidden in the middle circle, the circle of *Thinking*. Her second rune is ᚠ *feoh* in the circle of *Doing*. The third rune is ᚦ *thorn* in *Is*, outside the other circles.

The circles help us to pinpoint each rune more clearly. *Rad,* which we know is concerned with a hard but exciting change, is in Ellie's thoughts but she is finding it hard to make any positive steps in the real world, so it all goes round and round in her mind. There are hidden fears about failure and giving up the known if frustrating world.

Feoh suggests that the price she must pay for this change is a very real one. If she wants to turn a hobby into a career she will have to cope with opposition from her parents, a financial risk and all the new demands that will be made on her if she works for herself. But she is still young and it will be much harder to get off the financial treadmill once she has a mortgage.

The third rune, *thorn* in *Is* is perhaps the key. The small irritations are there and building up, making her feel trapped, the sameness of the job, the lack of scope for change in it and the complaints of the customers. Now may not be the time, but the problem is if she doesn't do something about her trapped feeling and try to melt the ice then she may well end up acting in a completely over the top way out of sheer frustration; maybe even walking out on her secure job over something trivial rather than leaving as a carefully planned step. What do you think Ellie's runes are saying? Tomorrow you can read your own cast.

Take out the three runes without looking and cast them. Now everything has got a place. Note the position of the three runes on your circle chart and mark which are hidden. If they are all very close, then you don't need me to tell you they are related. Can you make up any sort of story from the runes that makes sense in your life? Go back over the chapters and the summaries as many times as you like. There are no prizes for being first past the post. The only real prize is the self-knowledge and the will to shape your own destiny.

The cast of three

The central circle *Being* talks about the core issues, the real you. Runes falling here touch on pretty important issues. If the rune is hidden or the circle empty, perhaps you are a bit out of touch with what matters to you as opposed to other people. The runes will soon cure this.

Summary

If runes fall in the second circle *Thinking*, (thoughts, fears, hopes etc) they stand for issues that are much on your mind. If they are hidden then you may be living too much in your head and not translating the plans into the here and now.

The outer circle *Doing* is the area of your everyday world. Runes here tend to deal with current preoccupations. If hidden, then you keep getting crossed wires or criticism.

Is is the area outside the circles. Runes here mean you are stuck. If hidden then you may be frustrating yourself.

Hidden runes can show that you are not facing the issue. Clusters (groups of runes), falling together, are dealing with the same issue.

Runes covering each other indicate that one thing is dominating or distorting another.

In under two weeks you have learned all you need to know to enable you to read the runes for the most satisfying customer of all – yourself; though it is sometimes fun to peep into other people's circles. Now all you have to do is learn the rest of the runes, but as we do so we will be using them all the time, making our fortune, predicting and then shaping our own destiny. Oh, and don't forget the magic.

Gyfu is the rune of giving. The old meaning was also giving and though nowadays we don't hand our loved ones blood-axes wrapped in tinsel at Christmas and get a set of bone saucepans or a wooden CD in return, giving is still a very central issue to women. *Geefoo* is a good middle-of-the-road pronunciation that we can get our tongue round without upsetting the Great Runemaster too much.

Gyfu
The rune of giving

I was amazed that almost every woman seemed to turn up *gyfu* in her early readings, whether she was at college for the first time struggling on a grant, or aged 70 and wondering how she could manage on her pension. This is because giving, for women, is not primarily a financial issue, though many women, no matter how hard-up they are, will give their last penny to see other people's eyes light up at an unexpected treat.

Often, in the readings I did, *Gyfu* was hidden because giving can stir up some pretty primitive emotions we'd sooner keep the lid on. Woman is the provider of hot bison stew, the carer, nurturer of every lame duck who waddles to her door, but – who gives to the woman? *Gyfu* in a reading is very positive and creative: there are far fewer mean women than men, and those women who *do* have locks on their emotions as well as their purses often had bad experiences early in life that dried up this natural fountain of giving. At a time when you are being asked to give a lot, it is important to set limits that will not leave you feeling resentful.

When *gyfu* is hidden we need to take time to examine what we are being asked to give. Giving to our children and resenting it, or demanding love or lifeblood in return, is destructive to all concerned, even when such giving is due to unhappiness in the mother and not to any malice. Giving to ageing parents out of guilt in order to repay the debt they say we owe them is another destructive kind of giving. Giving to colleagues or in a relationship where it is all take by the other party can cause a woman of whatever age to feel taken for granted and undervalued.

A woman may need to examine not only the outward demands on her time but the hidden pressures – guilt, and her own need for approval and love – that seem to make her helpless before the demands of others.

Rune of the day

Start your rune of the day readings again. As you record them look over the past days and see if you notice any pattern emerging. This will be clearer as you use more runes.

Wyn, which looks like a sharp P is the rune of personal joy. Pronounced *win* like the prize it is, this is the hardest rune to write about and the least seen, especially in early readings. Mother, lover, housewife, sister, daughter, girlfriend, granny, personal assistant, charity worker, friend in need – the gyfu woman of the last rune. That is a very important aspect of a woman's experience, for she is a very person-centred creature. The fear of being alone and unwanted keeps many women on the straight and narrow, but ultimately frustrating, path.

But *wyn* is the other side of woman, one that is often forgotten during the hassle of balancing work and relationship demands. It is the joy that comes ultimately from ourselves alone. Remember those early teenage dreams and solitary wanderings? What makes you happy now you can no longer lie in bed till midday and dream away the hours? I'm talking about you, not you and the current love of your life, not you and the kids, your ageing relatives or grandchildren, not even you and your closest friends but YOU. What do you alone like doing or would like to do? What about the area where *they* end and *you* begin? The edges may be a bit blurred but can you make out the faint outline that is you? What do you like to eat, to read, to listen to? Take a few minutes out of servicing the world. Leave some domestic chore undone if you can't off-load it (unlikely unless the kids sprout wings and haloes). Opt out of those activities you go

Wyn
The rune of
personal joy

along to because you think you should but don't really enjoy, and use that time, however brief, to do something for yourself –or nothing at all if it will make you happy.

Wyn in a reading can tell you that just lately you've started to be aware of yourself as being separate from others. It's no bad thing to be realistic about even the most intense relationships and accept they can't and shouldn't meet all your needs. If *wyn* is still in your circle of *Thinking*, make this 'you' time happen in your everyday world.

If *wyn* is hidden, look at your fears of being alone and realise that this does not always equal being lonely or rejected. If you've had only bad experiences of being alone, start making small steps towards being on your own but doing something that makes you happy. Don't see these hours as being empty but as a fulfilling time spent with your very best friend: yourself. Ultimately, only if you are happy can you give happiness to others.

Don't forget to record your rune of the day at the back.

Haegel, which means hail, is sometimes regarded as a bad rune, and being caught in a hail storm isn't anyone's idea of a treat. But there are good and bad sides to everything and everyone, though we often try to push the darker bits into the cupboard. *Haegel* (pronounced *har-gool*) is the hassle rune, the rune of upsetting the applecart. (It's usually written *haegl*, but *haegel* is closer to the way it sounds.) But if the odd applecart is never upset, the *status quo* would stand in the way of change, often with all its injustices and apathy intact. And without constructive and beneficial change there can be no future, no fortune-making.

Haegel
The rune of
hassle

Saints, doormats, uncomplaining martyrs, their faces lined from the effort of keeping the fixed smile in place, avoid *haegel* like the plague. Use *haegel* loudly, clearly and unemotionally every time you hear the expression: 'You don't mind, do you?' as the world's dirty washing is dumped on your doorstep.

Of course you may find the hail is falling hard and fast on your head and you are constantly in the firing line of other people's battles; you are expected to act as the peacemaker in the family, or to listen to bitching friends who'd be better off with the RSPCA. If you are getting tired of waving the white flag while getting shot at in fights that have nothing to do with you, walk away. You'll be surprised how nice it is not to be walking around with all those bullet holes in you.

Borrow your offspring's personal stereo and play one of your tapes, or dig out the old battered record player from the attic and play a 78 from your teenage years and sing away for all you're worth. Go to the cinema, take the dog for a walk, shut your eyes and think of beautiful meadows or waterfalls or whatever makes you feel relaxed and secure. If there's nowhere else, sit on the loo till it's all over.

If you get *haegel* in a reading, the chances are that you're standing in the way of a lot of hassle from others. Leave them to fight their own battles or better still start a bit of *'haegel'* of your own and tell them to go play soldiers in the fast lane of the motorway.

If *haegel* is hidden in a reading, maybe you're putting up with things because you are afraid to cause any hassle. State firmly, but politely, that you *do* mind, whether it's your nearest and dearest or senior at work who's doing the asking, and then draw up what is reasonable to you.

Day 17

Edwina's cast of three

It's fun to play clairvoyant and eavesdrop on someone else's reading occasionally. But we must remember we cannot predict or shape their destiny any more than they can ours. We'll be using the circle now for any casts we do.

Edwina is in her late fifties and works part-time. She finds herself increasingly expected to take care of her four-year-old granddaughter on her days off and three or four evenings a week while her daughter and husband go out. Edwina's husband resents his wife babysitting as he wants her to accompany him to the social club where he spends his evenings, but he won't say anything himself. Edwina is constantly tired but feels she should help her daughter out. At the same time she doesn't enjoy the social club that much but doesn't want to upset her husband.

Edwina cast ✕ *gyfu* hidden right in her circle of *Being*, ⋈ *haegel* hidden in her circle of *Thinking* and ᚹ *wyn* in *Is*, (on ice) outside the other three circles. I read the hidden *gyfu*, as being right at the heart of the matter.

Edwina's reading

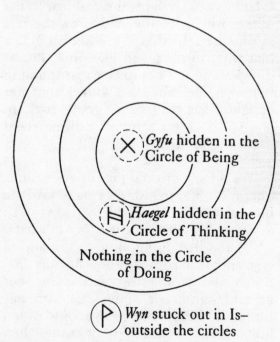

(✕) *Gyfu* hidden in the Circle of Being

(⋈) *Haegel* hidden in the Circle of Thinking

Nothing in the Circle of Doing

(ᚹ) *Wyn* stuck out in Is– outside the circles

Edwina feels she ought to be a good mother and grandmother and give to everyone else because she does have free time in the day and evenings when she can help her daughter out. She also feels that as a good wife she should go with her husband to the club though she doesn't enjoy it. But in the process of all this there is no-one considering her feelings.

Haegel is hidden in her circle of thoughts.

She is afraid of kicking up a fuss and limiting the help she offers her daughter and also of risking her husband's annoyance if she says she doesn't enjoy their evenings out. What is the real fear? That others will voice the criticisms she lays against herself: that she is selfish and a bad wife, mother and grandma. But as things stand she has to face disruption to her own life. She also knows that her daughter has got used to gran's back-up and will kick up a fuss if Edwina starts imposing limits.

Wyn – her personal joy rune – is stuck out on *Is* – waiting for Edwina to take the blowlamp to it. What does Edwina need to give to herself? Time to discover what it is she *does* like doing, time to rest and to enjoy her own company occasionally. She doesn't want to stop caring for her granddaughter or going out with her husband (though maybe she could widen his horizons), but she wants time when she isn't on call. Where does she get the time? By cutting down her babysitting duties and limiting the nights she goes to the club with her husband. The crucial difference is her time isn't divided between work and the conflicting demands of others but includes periods when Edwina does what she wants – or nothing. It won't be easy and the modern granny finds that she is often torn between the demands of grandchildren and her own needs.

Would you read Edwina's runes differently? There are no right or wrong answers remember – only Edwina has the power to choose how she will interpret the message and act on it.

Your cast of three

Now choose three runes without looking and cast them on your cloth. Note the position and name of each rune and mark it on the chart. Compare it with your last cast of three. Is it saying the same or have you moved on? Don't worry if you feel you aren't getting a lot at first – a few pointers at this stage are quite enough. The important thing is to get to know your runes and to use them. The rest will come. Don't forget to do your rune of the day. As you make more runes, these readings will reveal more about what is going on inside.

Summary

✕ *Gyfu* is the rune of giving. It can indicate that you are being asked to give a lot, but this can be very fulfilling so long as you set your limits. If *gyfu* is hidden then maybe you are giving out of unnecessary guilt and should give to yourself more.

ᚹ *Wyn* is the rune of joy and separateness. It may indicate that lately you have begun to realise that other people can't bring you total happiness. Explore and enjoy the uniqueness of yourself.

If *wyn* is hidden, perhaps you are afraid of being alone and abandoned. Try to do nice things when you are alone and discover your best friend – yourself.

ᚻ *Haegel* is the rune of hassle and upsetting the applecart. It may be telling you that you are at the centre of someone else's running battle and getting shot at for your pains. If *haegel* is hidden then perhaps you are too afraid of upsetting people by saying no. Tip a few apples out at first – you might get a taste for turning over apple carts completely.

Day 18

Nyd
The rune of need

At first *nyd* (which is pronounced —and means — *need*) very rarely appears in the centre circle (the ring of *Being*) because very few women are in touch with their real needs. That is hardly surprising. The need for approval, to be a good girl, is drummed into you from the very day when you're made to share your rusk with the baby boy waving his rattle menacingly at you. So we learn that the needs of others are always more important than our own. Even in supposedly liberated times, it is the guys in class who hog the computers and the girls who step back and later get accused of not being interested in modern technology.

Women often get *nyd* together with *gyfu*, usually hidden, because what you need and what you are given are usually very different but very closely linked. A woman once said to me: 'I give to other people what I need to be given by others but never get.' *Nyd* and *gyfu* are remarkably similar in shape and are often mistaken for each other. I often think *nyd* is *gyfu* (giving) squashed out of shape.

Nyd in a reading can indicate the strength of your own needs and where they really lie. Listen to them and try to put them ahead of other people's needs for a while; only if your needs are met (and you may end up having to meet a lot of them yourself) can you satisfy the needs of others without becoming bitter and disillusioned.

If *nyd* is hidden, you are denying your needs. Accept you have as much right as anyone else to happiness whatever you were told in your pram. So start banging *your* rattle.

Day 19

Is
The rune of ice

Is (pronounced *eess*) is the ice which we've already met as the place where your runes land if they're not on the cloth. Here is the rune, rather like an I, which means ice: it's like being ice-bound. *Is* in a reading will probably mean that you are waiting and unable to move forward. Usually someone else is holding you in this position. So all you can do is accept the situation and save energy by trying not to force your way forward.

If *is* is hidden, then maybe you are bogging yourself down with your own fears of change and it is time to get your blowlamp out and melt yourself free. However, the hidden aspect may suggest that what is bogging you down isn't obvious or you're not ready to move on yet.

When *is* falls in the realm of *Is* get a good book to read. You could end up stuck on this particular platform for quite a while.

Ger is the seasonal or treadmill rune. *Ger* rhymes with *air* and concerns the seasons of your life. There's not much hay-making in Clapham or Macclesfield, but wherever we live we women are much more aware than men of the cycles of our lives. What is important is accepting the natural inevitable changes of growing older. Life throws up many natural changes that can shake a woman to her core. A daughter's adolescence may coincide with a woman's own loss of fertility. Grandchildren and retirement are changes that can affect a woman much more deeply than a man because she sees changes in her physical body in a society that worships the young. But change has to be faced even for the younger woman: leaving school means that she is no longer protected. She may face the cruel dilemma of needing to be all things to all people: as successful as the boys, but also attractive to men. She finds that in spite of all the equality talk she heard at school, in the real world, in many professions, good looks are even today considered almost more important than a woman's abilities.

Ger
The seasonal or treadmill rune

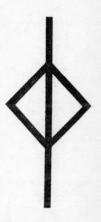

The younger female has just the opposite problem to the older woman: she has to look and act sophisticated in a very competitive world when all she feels like doing is going to bed with her teddy bear. Then once a permanent commitment has been made, the biological clock starts ticking away, and the most successful female executive can start peering in prams and taking sneaky trips round

Mothercare. The female life cycle can be cruel as well as creative unless we go with the natural flow and acknowledge our fears and regrets.

With *ger* in a reading, you may well be at a period of natural change in your life. It is only by accepting ourselves as we are at any stage and welcoming the new, though different, opportunities each change brings that we can be happy with ourselves.

If *ger* is hidden, then we may well be on a treadmill, trapped by the patterns we adopted early on which usually weren't all that successful but were all that was on offer at the time. We have met the old scripts in other runes so we find ourselves making the same mistakes time after time throughout out lives – only the people change. Try to see what it is you do that makes you say: 'Oh no, I've been here before and didn't like it then.' Use your runes to help you make a new movie.

Day 21

Linda's cast of three

Linda is in her fifties and works as a counsellor. But her own life is less successful and she keeps finding herself betrayed and hurt by close friends of both sexes who tend to be in their twenties. She will embrace new friends wholeheartedly and give them the coat off her back. Then she finds them taking over her life; she becomes resentful, but says nothing. Before long a new friend has conned her out of money or told Linda's most intimate secrets to the world. 'Why?' asks Linda.

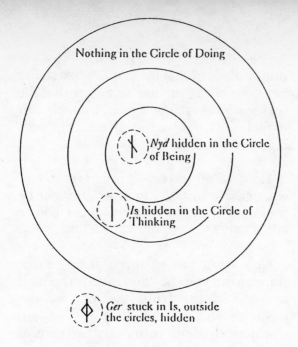

Nothing in the Circle of Doing

Nyd hidden in the Circle of Being

Is hidden in the Circle of Thinking

Ger stuck in Is, outside the circles, hidden

Linda throws ϕ *ger* hidden in the realm of *Is*. The rune | *is* is itself hidden in her circle of *Thinking* and $\uparrow$ *nyd* is hidden in her centre of *Being*. The first rune is perhaps the most significant.

She is well and truly stuck in choosing the same type and age of friend to satisfy a hidden *nyd* which is at her very centre and so is very important.

Linda was a very beautiful woman and she found it very hard to accept her *ger* – time is passing and her beauty is now of a different kind. Linda is mistaking her real need for approval and love, with the need for flattery and the company of young people who can kid her she is still twenty.

Is, her sticking point, is in the way she thinks about herself. So perhaps facing her needs head on and accepting that the seasons have changed would enable her to melt the ice since she is, in effect, holding herself back.

How would you read Linda's runes and what advice would you give? It might be useful to read the chapter again before you answer.

Your cast of three

Now do a cast of three, taking three stones from your bag and casting them on to your cloth. Note the names, the positions and whether they are hidden. Compare this with your other two casts of three. Are your readings changing as you become more aware of the magic in yourself?

Summary

Ϡ *Nyd* is the rune of needs. It can indicate that your own needs are important at the moment and perhaps aren't being met. Put yourself at the top of the list for a change and remember you are your own best friend.

Hidden, *nyd* may suggest you are denying you have any needs. Stop feeling guilty or selfish if you aren't happy with the way things are.

Ι *Is* is the 'stuck' rune when things are on ice. It can mean that you have to accept that circumstances are stopping you from making progress. But the ice will melt.

Hidden, it can be saying that you may be keeping yourself in a situation because change can be painful.

◊   *Ger* is the rune of the seasons and also the treadmill. It can indicate a time of natural change in your life. Accept and welcome these changes – would you really want to be 15 again? Think of all those school dinners.

If *ger* is hidden in a reading, then you may be stuck in the old patterns and find you keep making the same mistakes.

Day 22

We've been rabbiting on about seeing what story your rune of the day is unfolding. Let's have a look at someone else's daily rune pattern to see the kind of things we should look for. We'll take the last nine days and try to home in on the story.

Veronica's rune of the day

Veronica is in her mid-thirties, has three children aged six, eight and thirteen and has recently married for the second time after a traumatic divorce following her husband's constant womanising and unwillingness to be responsible for the children. Joe, her second husband, was a bachelor and though he loves Veronica finds it hard to come to terms with the noise and mess of the kids. Even with her part-time job, Veronica just cannot make ends meet as her ex-husband pays little maintenance though he showers the children with expensive gifts on the rare occasions he sees them.

There seems to be a constant running battle between Joe and the children, especially the teenager, and Veronica finds herself in the middle; the children constantly play Joe off against her ex. Veronica has a permanent headache and frankly wishes she hadn't bothered and feels like just walking out and leaving them all to it.

Veronica's runes of the day over nine days are:

Day 1 ⋈ *Haegel*
Day 2 ▷ *Thorn*
Day 3 ⊬ *Feoh* (hidden)
Day 4 ▷ *Thorn*
Day 5 ◇ *Ger* (hidden)
Day 6 ✕ *Gyfu* (hidden)
Day 7 ⊬ *Feoh*
Day 8 ✕ *Gyfu* (hidden)
Day 9 ⋈ *Haegel* (hidden)

Veronica begins and ends on *haegel* though the second is hidden. Not surprisingly, Veronica is surrounded by a lot of hassle from other people, not least the running battle between her second husband and the children, fuelled by her ex and his lavish gifts. The hassle consists mainly of everyday irritations and quarrels over the way the children behave (*thorn* on day 2) and the tension is building up.

Veronica is already experiencing headaches. *Thorn* is repeated on day 4 showing that the irritations and petty battles are a continuous, wearing feature of Veronica's life. The hidden *ger* suggests that being 'put upon' is a characteristic of Veronica's life, maybe carried over from her first marriage. Most likely here, as many women do, she acted as peacemaker between her husband and children, so successfully that the kids think the ex is a super-hero. She should ask herself why she continues to take on the Cinderella role, especially as the handsome prince has turned into one of the warring peasants.

Gyfu is hidden on both day 6 and day 8, showing that Veronica is perhaps giving all the time because she feels not to do so would make her a bad mother and wife and would result in her second husband leaving the nest, as did his predecessor. She has unrealistic expectations, based perhaps on the popular image of the happy family and feels responsible because hers (like 95 per cent of real life units) have more brickbats than bouquets.

Day 7 brings *feoh*, the price of continuing the way things are: hassle from her husband, her children and ex. Of course there is the underlying price: losing the approval of her children and maybe the presence of her husband, who has found the realities of family life so different from his solo existence and his own idealised picture of the happy family.

The final hidden *haegel* on day 9 suggests that Veronica does fear saying enough is enough to the opposing armies.

What do you think Veronica's daily reading is indicating? Maybe she needs to go off as she planned, not into the sunset, but well out of the firing line. For while she is taking the impact of the bullets, no-one else is likely to give in and make the necessary changes in their behaviour. Of course, it is never easy when a step-parent moves into a family, especially when the absent father, who previously may never have given the children a kind word, becomes, on his departure, the provider of goodies.

If the children are old enough to be manipulative, they are old enough to carry through the consequences of their behaviour, and Joe too will only rub into family life if he is exposed to it. It may not have a happy ending – real life often doesn't – but until Veronica gives up her role of peacekeeper the cycle cannot be broken.

Keep doing your own rune of the day readings. Try taking the most recent nine, including today's, and see what is emerging.

Eoh (pronounced *yo* as in *yo-yo*) refers to the yew tree and is the 'rune of limitations'.

That sounds pretty gloomy but, in fact, *eoh* is a very useful rune which speaks of putting aside those unrealistic expectations that may be keeping us from living life as it is.

Eoh
The yew tree
– the rune
of limitation

These unrealistic expectations keep the fortune tellers in business, but have no real place in fortune-making that starts from where we are and uses what we have on which to build. Let's face it: Prince Charming has gone to the wrong house with the glass slipper, so why stay at home waiting for him to call? *Eoh* suggests the ending of those inappropriate dreams. It may be a wrench but accepting the limitations means no more wasted energy dreaming of the impossible. It is very hard to look in the mirror and not imagine the 'after' picture when we've lost three stone and shed 20 years with that magic diet which secretly we know we shall not go through with. But you need to stop looking for this image and stop dwelling on the 'before' picture – when you were 17 and knew all the answers and weren't ever going to end up married, harassed, saggy and frayed round the edges like poor old mum.

Even if you are 17 you can still be bound by limitations. You've thrown away all those teen magazines with the boy meets girl stuff and you realise that the life of your mother isn't a million miles from your own. The grand career you planned as a nuclear physicist looks more like becoming a job in the local chemist, and all the boys at school who were going to be different and backpack round the world are settling down into a pattern not unlike your dad's.

But it's not that bad, even with no crown on your head and no sports car outside the door. You can be happier realising your limitations, acknowledging your achievements and knowing exactly who *you* are.

Eoh in a reading can indicate a dream shattered. All those youngsters in the fast lane are zooming past while you're chugging along in your Lada. You now realise that the chap who walked out on you three months ago isn't coming back with a bunch of red roses and a diamond ring. So you're feeling a bit battered and very disappointed. Youth or age, the knocks are just as hard. But remember you need an ending before you can go on to make a real beginning. And now you know there's no-one waiting in the wings, you can start to think how you are going to make it happen whether you want to be a nuclear physicist or a jet-setting gran.

If *eoh* is hidden, look a bit harder in that mirror. Go on – a proper look! You are hanging on to the regrets and the promises of tomorrow. No more soppy romances, no more soap operas for a while – write your own story and give yourself a happy ending.

Peorth, (pronounced like an upper crust version of *pay-off*) has many old meanings. It was the name of the rune cup used in casting lots, when the ancients were trying to decide whether to gallop off into the sunset and conquer another country or two before tea. It can also mean a tune, fate etc. But where does that leave us when dragging complaining toddlers round the supermarket or squashed on the train back to the suburbs after a fruitless day at the office? *Peorth* is the 'grass roots' rune: the real 'you' without the window dressing, with all your good bits, bad bits and wobbly bits, the real, central core person that hasn't changed all that much since you had plaits and will still be you when you are a cantankerous old lady.

Peorth
The essential you

If you were a bottle of perfume, *peorth* would be called *Essence of You*: roses and washing up liquid and car oil all mixed into one. This is the 'you' that makes brilliant jokes, cries over *Lassie* films, screams at the kids but would tear apart bare-handed anyone who touched a hair on their heads.

Peorth has sometimes been called (by the more elevated runesters who veer to the psychological), your 'inner child'. Indeed some of the more enlightened breed of psychologists will, for a sum of money, happily help you dig this bit out and tell you what you are saying. But you can easily find this bit using your runes. The part where those gut feelings that are always right come from is *peorth*. The runes, like the lager in the advert, can refresh those bits of you that other methods can't, because you, after all, know yourself better than anyone.

Peorth can let you know that a lot of bull has been flying around but you can see through it. You do know what to do – just follow that gut feeling and let your inner voice speak for you. If *peorth* is hidden then you may have been pleasing other people for so long you can't remember what you think and believe, or even if you still exist. If people are telling you different things, ignore them all.

What would you do left to your own devices? That is your answer.

Eohl
Your higher self rune

This is a heavy trio. The third rune *eohl*, your magic rune (also called *eohl-secg*) has meanings as wide apart as eel, elk and eelgrass. *Yole* to rhyme with *hole* will do as a pronunciation to stop the Great Runemaster hurling boulders at us. Psychics call this bit of us the 'higher self'. Do we have one? Most people get worried at this point and rely on tapes of bird-song and flowing waterfalls in an attempt to uncover this very special bit. Or they go to clairvoyants who then use their own *eohl* to enable them to have a stab at uncovering yours.

But how do you recapture this higher self? Let's go back to Santa Claus' Grotto when you were about five and didn't realise the magic wood backed on to the shoe department of the store. If you've had kids, remember the time after the 'never again' bit of giving birth when you looked into the eyes of the bundle in your arms and knew you were really in love for the very first time? Or what about the first time you fell in love, when the sun shone and the birds sang and you swore undying love by the deserted stream (not knowing a Scout troop was surveying the woods on the opposite bank). Who needs tapes about pretend waterfalls when you've had the real thing?

Whether 18 or 80, we've all got this magic bit that makes up the trio of our personal runes (remember *cen* and *peorth*?). Well *eohl* is the bit which joins you to the stars, the part that makes you know when your husband has pranged the car 40 miles away and makes you say, 'I told you that would happen', because you'd had a feeling that he should take the train and he'd ignored you. Or you phone mum from the other end of the country at ten o'clock at night because you know she's upset and she's right in the middle of a row with your dad. I didn't say anyone would be very pleased when you started using your magic powers (unless you can manage to provide the 3.30 winner at Kempton Park, people aren't usually interested).

Eohl has nothing to do with ghosts or spirits, so don't get any ideas of levitating along the street. It's the sort of magic that enables you to cut out the middle stages and know the answer – which is why many men have problems with *eohl*. It can be met in dreams, daydreams or flashes of inspiration or a feeling of certainty. It's different from a gut feeling in that it seems to come suddenly into your head.

To reach your own special magic just be still and quiet. I know its hard when there are hordes of kids (or you're sharing a college house with 20 intellectual elephants) but find a place, a time when you can be on your own (remember we peeped at this on day 1 when we were trotting along the beach or across the rec looking for pebbles?). You could even try an early morning walk. Yes, it is hell to drag yourself out of bed, but even the most urban setting is incredibly improved in the soft dawn light. Do nothing. Think of nothing. Let your feet plod along. You may remember a flash of what seems to be a past life – don't panic. It doesn't matter if it's true or not, enjoy it and see what it's saying about now.

If you get *eohl* in a reading then a logical approach to your problem isn't getting you very far. Get away from it for a while, don't think about the pros and cons – inspiration will come.

If *eohl* is hidden then you are perhaps depending on other people to give you the magic answer. Trust your own magic.

Pauline is in her forties and her husband left her for a younger woman after 20 years of marriage. She was devastated and spent hundreds of pounds on clairvoyants over the following five years trying to find out when her husband would return. She is still waiting.

Pauline's cast of three

Pauline casts ⟨rune⟩ *eoh* hidden in *Is*. ⟨rune⟩ *Eohl* was hidden in her circle of *Being* and ⟨rune⟩ *peorth* was hidden in *Is*. The key rune is perhaps *eoh*. Pauline is well and truly stuck in the regrets of yesterday and the hopes of her husband returning. Only she can melt this block of ice in which she has frozen herself.

Pauline's reading

Pauline has handed over her *eohl*, her intuition and inspiration, to the clairvoyants though she could answer her own question, 'When will he return?'. Until she takes this step the question that is central to her existence will remain unanswered. She needs to trust this intuitive side of her nature, probably much-under-played in her marriage and take the first brave step into the unknown. Maybe instead of pouring money into the pockets of clairvoyants she should go to a travel agent and book herself a nice holiday. Probably there won't be a handsome prince waiting but she might see new places and make new friends.

Pauline has got *peorth* to help which is also stuck in *Is*. Again she needs to free herself and find the real 'grassroots Pauline' brave and sensible who can start again, the Pauline who existed before and separate from her marriage and who is just waiting to be let out of the straitjacket. She must see this as the basis of a new future, for as long as we have ourselves we are never alone.

Pauline has two of her personal runes batting for her. The answer, it would seem, is in herself. What do you think? No-one is saying it's easy. Tomorrow we are going to do our first cast of six for ourselves. For now do just your rune of the day and add it to your ever unfolding story.

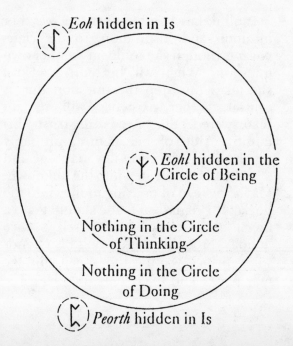

Eoh hidden in Is

Eohl hidden in the Circle of Being

Nothing in the Circle of Thinking

Nothing in the Circle of Doing

Peorth hidden in Is

ʃ *Eoh*, the limitations rune, can indicate disappointments but it can also help clear the ground to go forward. If *eoh* is hidden then you are still waiting for the handsome prince 25 years on. Come out of the ivory tower and get on with life.

ʞ *Peorth* is the grassroots rune, the real you without the window dressing. If you get *peorth* in a reading, the chances are someone's been trying to blind you with science. Trust your gut feeling. *Peorth* hidden may suggest that you have accepted other people pulling your strings.

Ⱡ *Eohl* is the magic 'you' that 'knows' what is going to happen, not through logic but inspiration. It can tell you that you've come up against the insoluble and that it's time to take a leap into the dark. You'll be all right. *Eohl* hidden means you've been relying on others for the magic answer. They've probably been off beam. Try your own magic. The runes will help you.

Day 27

This sounds complicated but all it consists of is two casts of three. So you'll take your three stones out of the bag, throw them on to the cloth, note the position on your circle chart at the back and then repeat the whole thing again. The only extra thing to remember is that if stones are close (in clusters) they are linked and stones on their own are a bit out of touch.

Casting six runes

Jackie is in her early forties and pregnant for
the first time. She and her partner have a very
comfortable life with plenty of foreign travel.
When they were first married he had said he
wouldn't mind a baby some day, but when
Jackie didn't get pregnant he refused to go for
tests and assumed that they would never have
children. Now there is a baby on the way he
says it will ruin their life and she should have
an abortion. Though Jackie greatly enjoys her
career as a journalist she is thrilled at the
chance of having a child when she had given
up all hope, and feels that, in spite of the
changes it will bring, it is the next step for her.
So Jackie does a cast of six.

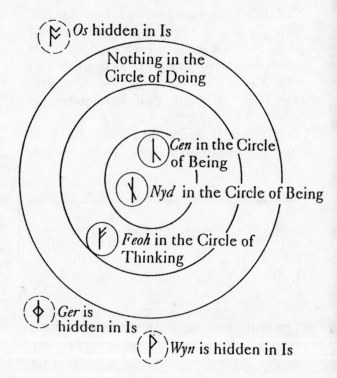

Os hidden in Is

Nothing in the
Circle of Doing

Cen in the Circle
of Being

Nyd in the Circle of Being

Feoh in the Circle of
Thinking

Ger is
hidden in Is

Wyn is hidden in Is

Rune 1	ᚠ	*Feoh* is cast by Jackie in the circle of *Thinking*	*Jackie's reading*
Rune 2	ᚵ	*Ger* is hidden in *Is*	
Rune 3	ᚾ	*Nyd* is in the circle of *Being*.	

So let's look at the first half of Jackie's cast of six. *Feoh*, the price, is in the second ring of thoughts, hopes and fears. The cost of either going ahead with the baby and accepting a changed life, perhaps without her husband, or giving up the chance of having a baby must be going round and round in Jackie's thoughts.

Rights and wrongs don't come into the runes, but what people feel and believe do.

Ger, the treadmill rune, hidden in *Is*, reflects the feeling Jackie has of being stuck in a sterile existence. Furthermore, she sees that having a baby is the next natural stage of her life. If she goes against what is for many women the natural ticking of the biological clock and the desire to have a child, it may ultimately destroy her relationship with her husband, because she will feel he has robbed her of a natural progression in her life. It is the dilemma of the modern working woman who suddenly finds, like her mother and grandmother, that a point can come when the call of biology becomes too strong to ignore.

Nyd, the rune of needs, is right in Jackie's centre. She can't see her own needs clearly right now but these are not being met although they are central to resolving the whole question. What she needs is the support of her husband, who fathered her child, and his protection during pregnancy when she feels vulnerable. It may be that her need to be protected and cared for hasn't been met in the marriage, where she has always acted as an equal partner or even unconsciously mothered her husband. What she wants and needs must ultimately be the deciding factor.

Rune 4 ᚠ *Os* hidden in *Is*
Rune 5 ᚹ *Wyn* hidden in *Is*
Rune 6 ᚴ *Cen* in her centre of Being.

Nothing is actually happening in Jackie's everyday circle. Now is the time for sorting out the past actions and for making plans for the future.

There is a lot of *Is* around – not surprising as Jackie is in a state of shock. When things are really bad, staying put and doing and saying nothing is sometimes no bad course. *Os* (communication), is hidden, and stuck.

No-one is talking about the real question – and certainly not answering it – which is, what basis for the marriage could remain if Jackie has an abortion?

Hard though it is, Jackie needs to listen to what her husband is saying and, of course, to express her own needs that were hidden in rune 3.

Wyn (the rune of joy) might seem a surprising one to pop up, but it is saying that for Jackie her personal happiness is now centred on the life growing inside her, a strange concept when children are often viewed as the end of personal freedom. But here we are talking about Jackie putting her own (and the baby's) happiness above her husband's desire for a free and easy life and especially above the relationship staying the same. It would seem that Jackie will, if necessary, go it alone rather than give up the chance of motherhood.

Cen (the inner voice) in Jackie's centre says that when all the pain has subsided a little, she has the answer if she will only listen to herself and draw both on her gut feelings and her inspiration (*peorth* and *eohl*) who will speak to her and tell her what to do.

Ultimately this advice from within is better than that which a hundred therapists, friends or clairvoyants can offer. The baby is her decision for it is growing in her body and no one should make the decision for her as to whether to go ahead with the pregnancy.

It may be that, faced with the choice of losing Jackie, her husband will do a little bit of growing up himself and support his wife in what she decides. Or, it may be that he will go off to find another supportive environment for himself. But if he forces Jackie to give up the baby, then the reality of the relationship may well be destroyed. The runes don't promise happiness, only that you are making the crucial decisions yourself and at the end of the day, if you have peace in yourself, you are never alone, however rocky the path.

Your cast of six

Now try your own cast of six. You can do these twice a week (any more is like weighing yourself every half-hour on a diet). If you are in a hurry or need an extra reading that is more detailed than your rune of the day, then do a cast of three. You are in charge, so use the runes to fit in with your life, not your life to fit the runes.

Day 28

Sigil
The 'go for it' rune

Sigil, the 'go for it' rune, is pronounced *see-gel* (also written as *sigel*). It is the old sun rune and is the key to all the dreams you could still attain – don't forget if you are older these now include many things you could not have done as a teenager, no matter how self-confident you were. For now you've got experience, understanding and had all those awkward corners well and truly knocked off. *Eoh*, the reality rune, made you accept that you aren't going to get a handsome prince with a bag of money knocking at the door.

But if you are just starting out then the dreams are those you haven't yet unfolded and perhaps are wondering whether it is worth bothering. Is it worth moving to a job that affords promotion at the other end of the country when it means leaving the crowd you've gone round with since the first day of school? Is it worth the financial struggle to train for three years as a social worker or teacher when everyone else is getting good money with the minimum of hassle even if their jobs would drive you up the wall with boredom?

Sigil says that whatever your age or marital status there is so much you can still do, even given the limitations of your time and circumstances. If you really want to do something go for it, and ignore the people who try to put you down to boost their own egos.

It doesn't have to be evening classes or things that you feel you ought to do to be a success in the world's eyes. Nor do you need to learn meditation and wander through imaginary fields of buttercups to find those parts of yourself that you can already reach while peeling the potatoes or cleaning the communal bathroom. *Sigil* is about developing your unique gifts that your life has given you.

If you get *sigil* in a reading, don't let anything stand in your way. If you have children, let the family have unironed clothes and eat junk food, while you free yourself from the daily grind for a change to do what you want. If you are solo, then don't let the discouragement of others or inertia hold you back.

If *sigil* is hidden in a reading then you are probably feeling vaguely dissatisfied at providing the back-up service for everyone else's action. Decide what you want to do with your life and go for the prize.

Day 29

Tir
The sacrifice rune

Tir (pronounced *tear* to rhyme with *beer*) is the 'sacrifice' rune. The idea of sacrifice summons up images of a tight-lipped mother producing Christmas dinner for 25, in a kitchen no bigger than a shoe-box in temperatures that make Hell's Mouth seem positively icy, or an older single woman giving up her life and independence to care for an elderly relative. Even the young are not immune. How many young women have given up the chance of a better job to stay close to a boyfriend or have given up a college place because it would involve leaving mum on her own? Women make sacrifices every day, some appreciated, some without even a word of thanks in return.

But *tir* is to do with making an immediate sacrifice for a long-term improvement in your life. *Tir* was the god who sacrificed his hand to save the other gods from the giant wolf who threatened to swallow the world. Legend has it that the other gods were not particularly appreciative of his efforts but thought it rather amusing that he had lost his hand in the struggle to bind the wolf. From our first day as Brownies, and ever after, we are taught that it is noble to sacrifice ourselves for the good of others. But by the time you've thrown your guide's beret into the nearest duckpond you've probably stacked up enough good deeds to last a lifetime, and can start thinking about whether your sacrifice can be of benefit to you personally as opposed to a load of ungrateful gods, stroppy teenagers or complaining colleagues.

Perhaps you have been running the office for ten years on a fraction of the boss's pay and with none of his perks. So you decide to take a business course. But first comes the sacrifice bit. To achieve that you are going to have to sacrifice the comfort of *not* carrying the can when things go wrong. You will have to give up those evenings slumped in front of the telly or at the wine bar and force your screaming mind and aching body to go on courses and read books. *Tir* implies you are choosing to make a sacrifice, but that, if you do, the rewards will be tremendous.

If you get *tir* in a reading, then you are perhaps on the verge of a new stage in your life. It could be telling you that an initial sacrifice now will bring long-term improvements.

If *tir* is hidden, then you may have been giving up too much for other people. Giving up 'giving up' could be your first positive sacrifice.

Day 30

Beorc
The rune of relationships

Beorc (bay-ork), the birch or poplar, is often associated with the goddess of hearth and home. It focuses on the important relationships in your life. For a woman, close relationships are an important part of her world. Women tend to be the glue that keeps families together (even if the families are at each other's throats). Left to themselves, males tend to wander off or tear one another limb from limb. And it's not only the older woman who gets lumbered. It's often the teenage girl who is round to visit gran on a Sunday. Brother, of course, is at the match or weight-training or brain dead in front of an arcade game.

But family relationships can stop us treating one another as real people. Because we are so close to our partner or family, we sometimes only relate to them by acting as mum, sister, daughter or wife and get locked into patterns that stop us from asking them to give us the consideration we would expect from friends.

Of course we need people with whom we can be bloody-minded, moody and miserable and whom we know will love us whatever. But then we can end up trapped or resentful because mother treats us as though we were naughty five-year-olds though we are 40 and president of a national bank. But we do continue to act out these old roles and end up hating our sister not because of what she is now (unpleasant though she may be) but because she was always Father's favourite and cut up our best doll when we were five.

If you get *beorc* in a reading, the chances are the family or your beloved is very much on your mind. Be sure you are dealing with the real person and the real issue and insist that you are recognised by partners and family as a mature adult not a child or inferior. Partners can be very sneaky about off-loading childhood rivalries on you or making you feel you are competing with his mother (and losing). Equally mothers can still see you as the stubborn four-year-old who spat her greens all over the cat.

If *beorc* is hidden then you may be the one playing the old games: daddy's girl or the martyred mother. Forgive and then change what can be put right. Let the rest go and then meet your family as people. You may well find you don't like them very much. Remember the old saying: you can't choose your family; be glad you have such nice friends.

ᚻ Sigil *(seegle)* is the 'go-for-it' rune, the rune of all your undeveloped potential; it can indicate the time is right for change. If *sigil* is hidden, then you are probably feeling frustrated at being the spectator all the time. *Summary*

ᛏ Tir *(tear)* is the sacrifice rune, of giving something up now for a long-term gain. It can suggest the right time to shed the comfortable old ways that keep you safe, but bored. If it is hidden, you may be making the wrong sacrifices.

ß *Beorc (bay-ork)* is the rune of close relationships with family or partner. It may be telling you to sort out old family rivalries and treat your family as real people not demons or plaster saints. If *beorc* is hidden, then you are trapped in the old games and need to see yourself as not just mum, wife, daughter but as a person in your own right.

Day 31

Sally's rune of the day

Sally is in her early 60s and has been a widow for many years; she has brought up her son to whom she is very close. Her son has recently married a New Zealand girl and intends to emigrate. Though Sally does not get on very well with her daughter-in-law, she has been invited to go with them. Sally has built up a network of friends and activities, but fears she will lose touch with her only family if she does not go. However, since she is retired and the couple will work, she is afraid of being alone in a strange country.

Day 1	ß	*Beorc* (hidden)
Day 2	Ո	*Ur* (hidden)
Day 3	Ρ	*Wyn*
Day 4	ß	*Beorc* (hidden)
Day 5	↑	*Tir*
Day 6	♦	*Ger*
Day 7	Ʀ	*Rad* (hidden)
Day 8	Ͷ	*Sigil* (hidden)
Day 9	ʃ	*Eoh*

Sally starts with *beorc*, hidden, which not surprisingly leads us into the family dilemma: should mum go or stay? It might seem that Sally has not quite accepted her son as grown-up and may, without realising it, be resenting her daughter-in-law because she has spoiled the closeness between mother and child. Of course, the daughter-in-law might actually be a rat-bag when Sally looks at her as a real person. But then Sally needn't feel guilty for not liking her.

Day 2 throws up the obstacle rune, *ur*. Sally has to overcome the very real fear she is hiding that once her son moves far away then she will lose touch with him completely (encouraged by daughter-in-law). Maybe she should talk this fear over with her son and his wife to see if there is a way of keeping in touch if she doesn't go with them.

Day 3 and *wyn*, the rune of joy, that comes from yourself, is a gentle reminder of the life Sally has built here apart from her family.

Beorc on day 4 is hidden again. The family is still pressing and it's the hidden issues that need to surface and be talked over now, rather than packing a load of resentments in a cabin trunk which could sour any new life.

Day 5 brings *tir* – the sacrifice for a long-term advantage. My guess would be that if she let her son and his wife go now with a smile, they would be grateful for the time to get established together without mum. They may return eventually or she could go later when they were established.

It's a gamble but she might find her daughter-in-law would appreciate her for this and perhaps feel less threatened.

Day 6 reveals *ger*, a reminder of the different stages of life and the need to accept and move on, in Sally's case maybe away from being mum. She is by no means too old to start a new life in a new country, if that is what she really wants, or perhaps to make a very happy, independent life here as she has already started to do.

Day 7 throws up a hidden *rad*, the rune of the rough ride, implying that Sally may be thinking of taking the soft option. For Sally, it would be easier to live with her son and wife and rely on them for company, rather than face the fear of being left alone thousands of miles away.

But in the long run she may find that it is harder having to start again from scratch without her network of friends and clubs she has here.

On day 8 the hidden *sigil* indicates that Sally still has many dreams unfulfilled and is still young enough to learn new things. She will also have the bonus of holidays in New Zealand with all the exotic stop-overs.

Day 9 gives her *eoh*, the acceptance of limitations and that one way or another there will be an ending, either leaving her life here or losing daily contact with her son and her effective role as mum. Only Sally can decide. If she does let him go, she may find there is an elderly knight in slightly rusty armour around the corner who may start courting her in his Morris 1000.

Now look at your last nine runes of the day. Can you see runes that keep cropping up or are always hidden? Is some sort of story unfolding?

Day 32

Eh (pronounced to rhyme with the *'em'* it resembles) is the rune of the horse. Of course you might take up riding or meet Steptoe with his junk-cart but that is not usually what *eh* signifies. For *eh* is the juggling rune, the rune of harmony and balance – the ancient warrior riding off on his horse, man and beast as one. Keeping all the balls in the air at once is no easy task with the conflicting pressures of work, home and pleasure (what's that?). You may be balancing old Aunty and stroppy son so she doesn't go home mortally offended and cut you out of her will. Or trying to stop your boyfriend from coming out with his views on the evils of capitalism in the middle of Sunday lunch, when it's your parent's materialistic tendencies that bought the roast beef he's tucking into.

Eh
The rune of balancing and harmony

But what about your harmony, that inner peace necessary for *cen* (the inner voice) to get a word in edgeways? Who ends up frazzled, distinctly unharmonious and, having soothed everyone else's troubled feelings, finally flips and is accused of being unbalanced? The unbalanced nature of woman has less to do with her hormones and more with the conflicts caused by trying to maintain the equilibrium of others.

Stop and make time for yourself, if it is only 20 minutes every day when you do absolutely nothing. Think nothing (we started talking about this when we were talking about *eohl*, our magic rune). Go for that walk, lie on the bed with ear-plugs in (having put the kids in front of the video with a bag of crisps – at this stage their systems can stand a bit of neglect more than yours). Or lock yourself in the communal bathroom and have a good soak without being tempted to clear up the mess first. Refuse to think about anybody or anything.

Eh can indicate you've been feeling a bit frazzled lately. Stop worrying about everyone else's happiness and the thousand things you haven't done. The world won't end if you're not at the wheel.

If *eh* is hidden, perhaps you've forgotten the most important person in your life: you. You could actually be fuelling the quarrels around you, whether with friends, family or workmates by leaping in with your white flag every time voices are raised. If there's no audience, (ie you) then family and office backbiting could lose its attraction for the combatants.

Man means man (the woman's bane and her support at the same time). This is the rune of strengths and weaknesses, both your own and those of others. Most women are brilliant at making allowances for the weaknesses of others and being remarkably honest about their own mistakes. But women underestimate their strengths and abilities and see others as more competent or able than themselves.

Man
The rune of strengths and weaknesses

This is all part of the put-down mentality that has been spoon-fed with the first rusks into baby girls. To counter this we need to identify our own special gifts. Write down anything you are good at, not just actual skills but virtues: stickability, patience, the ability to go to the heart of the problem, etc. Even weaknesses are, of course, potential strengths: stubborness is only strong principle attached to an unimportant cause.

Often we see others as happier, more organised than ourselves, but when you really talk to them, you find it's like a mirror and they thought you were Mrs or Ms Unflappable. Ms Perfect, that slim, always-smiling hub of the newly-laundered happy family that inhabits the land of TV adverts is just a myth, as is Ms Have-it-All who possesses the shiny sports car, glossy mane, gleaming smile and hunky male.

Those who put down others at every turn are the ones with the real image problem. Scratch the surface and you'll find the spiteful little girl who used to trip you up with her skipping rope in the school playground. Think of her like that and she'll lose the power to make you feel useless.

Man in a reading suggests you may have been enduring a lot of put-downs lately that have made you feel useless. Family, friends and colleagues at work often have an interest in keeping us in the down position on the see-saw. Make allowances for yourself when things do go wrong, and start to blow your own trumpet a bit.

If *man* is hidden maybe you have been playing down your own abilities to make others feel good. Mums especially tend to act stupid to make husband and children feel smart, and after a while even believe it. But women in general find it hard to crow about their achievements. Even if you've got a string of degrees as long as your arm, until you think you are great, no one else will.

Lagu (pronounced *largoo*) means water and is the rune of your feelings and emotions. Women are often accused of getting over-emotional; this usually happens when the man in your life has got himself into a corner and resorts to a bit of uproar so you won't notice he's made a fool of himself. Emotions are woman's greatest gift, the ability to be moved by the sorrow of others, to share the pain and distress of others, to sympathise with the world and generally feel what others are feeling.

Lagu
The rune of
emotions

Of course, unchecked, or not backed by action, all this emotion can get a bit soggy and ineffectual. But a woman's feelings on a subject are often a pretty good guide and can accurately sum up a situation in five seconds flat. Just learn to trust your feelings and accept that if you feel upset it is probably with good cause.

What about those feelings that aren't attached to a particular event but come from inside, as you feel time passing. Your negative feelings are equally important. If you feel sad about growing old, jealous of your teenage daughter or fed up with your mum taking her menopausal blues and grotty marriage out on you, then admit it to yourself and have a good cry or a private pillow-thumping session. Afterwards you'll find you have room for the happy feelings that have been dampened down by the weight of your anger or sadness. Let your kids see you get upset about things, and about them when they are foul.

To display to your children an ever-smiling, loving image can create dreadful problems for them; they feel that they are bad because they experience feelings of anger or jealousy. To con a daughter-in-law that your relations with your son were perfect or that your marriage was all roses is unfair and, in the long run, unlikely to promote good relations. A sad mum may crack the plaster saint image, but it helps family members to accept their own shortcomings and admit their feelings. To insist that you are always in control and don't need anyone, creates barriers and cuts off a valuable source of support.

It is part of the modern con that women do not feel able to share their vulnerable side, but until we do, it is hard to bring out the caring side in our men.

Lagu in a reading shows you have probably been feeling pretty churned up by events. Trust your feelings and react accordingly.

If *lagu* is hidden, you've maybe been hiding your feelings too much. The ever-smiling woman sets impossible standards for others and a fixed smile can put dreadful lines on her face.

Tomorrow we'll try a cast of six for someone else and then you can do your own. Don't forget your rune of the day.

Summary ᛗ *Eh* is the juggling rune, the rune of harmony and balance. It may be telling you that you are feeling a bit frazzled and should make time for yourself. If *eh* is hidden, you may be fuelling disharmony around you by acting as interpreter and peacemaker.

ᛗ *Man* is the rune of strengths and weaknesses. It can tell you to blow your own trumpet more, because other people aren't appreciating you. If *man* is hidden, then you are playing down your own abilities to make other people feel good.

ᛚ *Lagu* is the rune which can tell you to trust your feelings. If it is hidden then perhaps you are trying to be too calm and controlled: let rip occasionally.

Day 35

Samantha's cast of six

Samantha, an only child in her mid-20s, still lives at home. As a result she has a very good lifestyle, nice car and holidays abroad. Her career is going nowhere, but her female boss recognises her potential and suggests she transfers to the Paris branch of the firm in six months' time when a vacancy arises, and that she should start going to French evening classes in preparation. However she has been warned that the cost of living in Paris is very high and the office a very competitive one as opposed to the laid back attitude that prevails in her present job.

Her parents are very unwilling to lose their only daughter's company and since they are comfortably off can afford to subsidise her.

Rune 1 ᛗ *Man* hidden in Samantha's circle of *Thinking*

Samantha's reading

Rune 2 ᛗ *Eh* hidden in her circle of *Doing*

Rune 3 ᚢ *Sigil* hidden in *Is*

Rune 4 ↑ *Tir* hidden in her circle of *Thinking*

Rune 5 ᛒ *Beorc* in *Is*

Rune 6 ᚱ *Lagu* hidden in her circle of *Doing*.

What a lot of hidden runes! Something's bubbling away down there in Samantha's hidden volcano in spite of her laid-back, cushy life. Given the high mortgage rate and difficulty of finding rented accommodation, many overgrown baby birds do linger in the nest and this is not without tension on all sides.

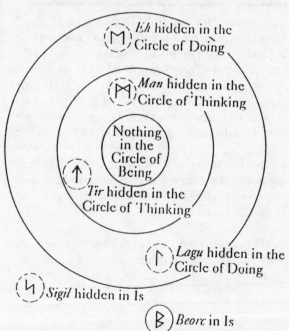

Eh hidden in the Circle of Doing

Man hidden in the Circle of Thinking

Nothing in the Circle of Being

Tir hidden in the Circle of Thinking

Lagu hidden in the Circle of Doing

Sigil hidden in Is

Beorc in Is

Rune 1 *man* is very central. Samantha has kept her own strengths and abilities well-hidden because neither her job nor her home life have given her any incentive to stretch herself. Now the job offer has made her think, perhaps for the first time, about expanding her horizons.

Eh, the harmony rune, tells us that Samantha is apparently in a harmonious situation and ironically it is the job offer that is threatening the domestic *status quo*. But we wonder whether Samantha has unconsciously been keeping the peace at home by not striking out and moving into her own place. Is the parental relationship dependent on Samantha's balancing act? What has it cost Samantha in ensuring a happy home by stifling her natural independence? The runes can dig up all kinds of things. Well, I said maybe there was a volcano bubbling away under the surface.

Rune 3, *sigil*, her 'go-for-it' rune of her own undeveloped ambitions, is hidden on ice. Her job is jogging along in an undemanding way, but fortunately her boss has recognised Samantha's potential and is offering her a way out of the rut.

Rune 4, *tir*, tells Samantha that achieving her unfulfilled potential will involve initial sacrifices on her part, not least giving up her well-feathered nest, living alone for the first time in a strange country and being short of money. Also she'll have to start evening classes which can be a real bind after a day at work. Plenty of candidates for *tir*.

But in return Samantha will eventually gain independence from her parents and the prospects of a good career.

Rune 5, the family relationship rune *beorc*, is again stuck on ice – not surprisingly. On one hand there are Samantha's parents trying to keep her well and truly their little girl and paying happily for the privilege. Then there's Samantha whose role as loving daughter seems central to her parents who perhaps only define themselves in the parenting role. So perhaps a physical move over the miles will give the necessary breathing space for the real people to emerge, though this will not be without pain.

Rune 6, *lagu*, the feelings rune in her everyday world, suggests that her parents are operating a degree of emotional blackmail and have perhaps kept Samantha from being able to express the normal teenage rebellion that eases the road to independence. So Samantha has to be prepared to cope with many emotions on both sides being brought into the open.

Your cast of six

Now do your own cast of six, remembering to draw the runes in your circle chart at the back and noting whether the runes are hidden or not? How does it compare with your previous casts of six? Are you hiding fewer runes or getting less on ice? Does the cast suggest the same things as before?

Ing is the rune of withdrawal, the 'take-one-day-at-a-time' rune. The rune of *ing* refers to a hero god taking himself off in the opposite direction to the sun, and maybe you've lately fought one too many battles.

Ing
The rune of retreat

Most likely you've suffered a loss, whether the end of an important relationship or just a temporary loss of confidence, perhaps prompted by being passed over at work, being betrayed by a friend or being told you are too old for a certain position. *Ing* tells us there is a time when we need to let everything be, and rest physically and emotionally.

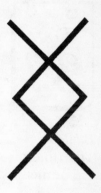

Do only the minimum for a while: easy meals, early nights. It is not a time to paint the house or take up assertiveness training. Let time heal and nurture you, grieve for whatever you have lost and accept that you feel awful. Don't worry about the future or even the past. Don't go rushing round trying to rewrite history or putting the world to rights. Leave it all till you are stronger. Grieve and then bury it, literally if you like - throw flowers off a bridge, stones into the water, say goodbye and then accept it – it's over. As far as possible see only people by choice who make you feel good.

Then one day you'll look out of the cave and notice it's stopped raining. But not yet.

If *ing* in a reading, the chances are you are feeling a bit bruised and battered. Wait, do nothing and let time take it's course.

If *ing* is hidden then you may be lashing out blindly, because you feel wronged, and you may end up hurting yourself most of all. The tanks are empty, for now you have no more to give. So don't try.

Day 37

Odal
The rune of the home

Odal (rhymes with *owed Al*. And is also called *ethel*.) It is the homestead, the bricks and mortar rune, the rune of the practical issues of your life. The nitty gritty of living might seem out of place with all this talk of inner voices and higher selves. But like all creatures from cockroach to queen bee, we need a base, a nest, a practical set-up from which we go forth to conquer the world and scuttle back when the going gets rough and we need a spell of *ing*.

We need to have a working routine without too many irritations, places to shop where we won't have to seethe two hours at the checkout, and transport that gets us from A to B when we need it to. All the inner harmonies and golden dreams ultimately stand and fall on these basic issues. Who does what, and how, are very practical issues on which marriages, families, house-sharing arrangements and careers can flourish and founder.

If you get *odal* in a reading, a lot of your time has probably been taken up lately with the practical issues of life. Maybe you are doing too many mundane things for other people while they are fulfilling their destinies and you are chained to the kitchen sink or coping with the boring routine jobs at work while others swan around and take the credit.

Now's the time to start getting your space, whether at work or at home, as you want it.

If *odal* is hidden in a reading, then too many domestic tasks or a heavy workload may have been caused by you accepting more than your fair share because you don't want to seem pushy or lose the approval of others.

Day
38

Daeg (pronounced *darg*) is the waking-up rune. This awakening sometimes happens when you've come out of your cave after a period of *ing* and found that the sun is shining. You can be 20 or 90 when enlightenment comes. It's not a once and for all 'conversion on the road to Damascus' experience, because life contains many seemingly endless tunnels. Some say the first heartbreak or the first loss is the worst because after that you

 learn there will be another day, another dawning. I am not convinced because there are new sorrows we aren't prepared for, as well as joys, waiting at every stage of life. But there are new *daegs* at the end of those dark times.

Daeg
the rune of
the dawning

Daeg is seeing the light in a situation you thought had no solution, the light at the end of the tunnel after a long hard slog. It's not a magical answer plucked out of the sky or dropped from the shopping basket of the Great Runemistress as she goes about her daily prophesying.

Daeg is the key to your fortune-making when you suddenly realise that you can make it, overcome the hassles and the wrong turns. You are not there yet, nor will you be for some time. Remember you're pedalling your own bike, not hitching a lift on a white charger. It will be quite a sudden realisation, a quiet confidence that whatever the other lot do or don't do, you'll be all right.

It's not the last piece in the puzzle, but the missing one. Now you've found it, you can see the shape and pattern. The whole thing makes sense. You may find *daeg* is hidden at first, because it's very dazzling to step out of the cave into the sunlight. So, though it is a sudden flash of understanding, you may need to go slowly till you are used to the light penetrating those cobwebby corners. And, of course, you may need many visits to the jumble sale with the clutter you've forgotten.

Daeg in a reading can bring you hope and help to signpost the way ahead. You know you're on the right track at last. If *daeg* is hidden in a reading, then the answer is there. Keep faith with yourself and you will get there.

Ing is the rune of withdrawal or **Summary** taking one day at a time. It may be saying that the only thing you can do is to walk away from whatever is hurting you and give yourself time to regain your strength. Hidden, it may indicate that you are lashing out at everyone but hurting only yourself.

◊ *Odal* is the 'bricks and mortar' rune dealing with the practical organisation of your life. It may be telling you that these issues are standing in the way of progress, so it's worthwhile sorting them out so that everyone takes a turn. Hidden it can mean that you are doing more than your fair share of the dirty work but don't like to protest. Why?

⋈ *Daeg* is the waking-up rune when the answer to your problem dawns on you. It can indicate that you are on the right path at last. If *daeg* is hidden then the last answer is there, very close to home.

Ac
The 'on
your bike'
rune

Ac (pronounced *ark*) is an oak (noted for its independence in the days when we could still chat to trees and not be locked up). It is the 'on your bike' or 'veto' rune, the straw that broke the camel's back.

We all have limits beyond which we can't be pushed even by those we love most.

You probably haven't seen a lot of *ac* in your life since you were 14 and tossed your silky locks at the boy you'd vowed to worship forever (well two weeks was a long time in those days).

'No way, sunshine,' you told him when he suggested a quick cigarette and grope behind the school bike-shed, and you went off to tell your best friend that all men were pigs and you'd never ever trust one again (a lot of sense we spoke at 14 without realising it!).

Since then we have become a lot wiser and learned to put up with a whole load of hassle before we finally draw the line and say 'on your bike' in our relationships. But every worm has its turning point and though you may be adaptable and peace-loving at work and in your family life, if pushed too far you will assert your independence (you may even see *peorth*, the real you popping out and taking over at the helm).

When you get *ac* in a reading, you will find that just lately people have been pushing their luck with you and you feel you can't stay silent and reasonable much longer. Good! Speak now and they will forever hold their peace – or at least take their hassle elsewhere.

When *ac* is hidden in a reading you are feeling threatened by a situation or person. Don't be brow-beaten. Remember that 14-year-old, who knew exactly what she was worth and what she was prepared to give. She is still there inside you if you need her. Call her and let her say 'on your bike' and watch your opponents shrivel.

Aesc (pronounced *ask*) – another tree, this time the ash. This tree has the reputation for stickability and is not surprisingly much more frequently seen than the previous rune. Endurance, making the best of things 'making do and mending' are all familiar concepts to a woman from the day she has to patch together her favourite poster, ripped up by her brother. *Aesc* can be a reminder that it is sometimes worthwhile hanging on during a rough patch till things improve. Of course there will be times when you need to be *ac* rather than *aesc* but here we are talking about those less dramatic situations that go on and on but aren't actually threatening sanity or life.

Aesc
The rune of endurance

It is interesting that the 'on the bike' rune should occur before the stickability rut I suppose the runes are saying: 'OK, it's not one of those major breaking points, not the tooth that has to be extracted but rather the gnawing ache that needs a filling.'

The present situation won't last forever so don't give up hope, although, if you are still young, waiting a year or even three years to get through a course or save the deposit for a home of your own may seem an endless struggle. If you are older you may find that you are tied by the children or infirm parents, or stuck with a job you don't enjoy in order to pay the bills.

If you get *aesc* in a reading, the chances are that you are finding life a bit of a slog. But that doesn't mean you can't improve things for yourself if only by accepting that you've got to stick at the present situation and enjoy whatever aspects you can while you're waiting. Or perhaps you can get ready for the time when you are able to make changes.

If *aesc* is hidden in a reading, then you may be running round in circles like a scalded cat trying to find a way out. This is taking up a lot of the energy that you need to keep you going. Accept the inevitable for a while and see what positive factors or helpful people there are in your situation that you can draw strength from.

Yr (pronounced *year*) means the bow that is made from the yew tree (we met the yew as *eoh*).

This is the rune of 'using all you have learned', the 'maturity' rune. Within yourself you have tremendous resources of wisdom and understanding that have come from all the experiences, good and bad, you have had in your life. Even if you are only 20 you have still faced many disappointments and come to terms with life outside the world of school and home. So you are not starting from scratch. You have lost the arrogance and irresponsibility of your early teens. You have had to learn to get along with people and accept their funny ways.

Yr
The
maturity
rune

You manage to fit in an incredible amount in your day and meet a thousand different demands, even if you get a bit frazzled in the process. You are kinder and more willing to admit you don't know it all. And this is a rune that actually improves with age, for the older you are, the more real achievements and insight you have to base your future on. It more than compensates for the decrease in actual physical energy.

If you get *yr* in a reading, then you may have been feeling a bit redundant and out of touch lately. Dig deep in yourself and you will find tremendous resources to fashion out a place for yourself in the world. Perhaps you need a change of scene to allow these resources to be used fully.

If *yr* is hidden in a reading, perhaps you are clinging to a redundant stage in your life that isn't enabling you to use all you have learned. Whether you are facing leaving home for the first time or coming to terms with your retirement, it is important to embrace the next stage using all you have learned and experienced.

Margery's cast of nine

Margery is in her late 30s and suffers from a progressive wasting disease. Since her divorce nine years ago she has had a series of live-in boyfriends and is in the process of splitting from the latest. In every case the problem is the same. At first she welcomes men who will care for her and protect her from the difficulties of life, but then she starts to feel stifled by their attention and longs to feel normal. Will she ever find Mr Right who will love her as a woman not an object of pity?

Her first three runes are:

Margery's reading

Rune 1 ᚻ	*Yr* in the centre of *Being*
Rune 2 ᚲ	*Ac* hidden in the realm of everyday, the circle of *Doing*
Rune 3 ᚪ	*Aesc* in the realm of everyday, the circle of *Doing*

Yr, the bow, the rune of resourcefulness, is in Margery's centre which suggests that she has the resources to improve her position, but is sitting around the house

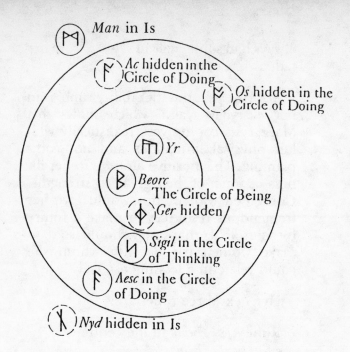

Man in Is

Ac hidden in the Circle of Doing

Os hidden in the Circle of Doing

Yr

Beorc

The Circle of Being

Ger hidden

Sigil in the Circle of Thinking

Aesc in the Circle of Doing

Nyd hidden in Is

feeling depressed, however understandable that may be. She is a very intelligent woman with an alert mind and this provides the key to the way forward: as her physical horizons narrow, perhaps she should take a college course or even a home study.

Ac, the oak, the rune of independence is hidden in her realm of everyday life, indicating that she is avoiding relying on herself perhaps because she knows her physical limitations. But this is the very quality that eventually kicks against the caring behaviour of her partners that she sees as smothering.

However, this is very difficult for her, not only because of her illness but because, by her own admission, she has always had some male to rely on from her father onwards.

Aesc, the ash, the stickability rune, is in her everyday realm, which shows that Margery is coping very realistically with her physical limitations and not complaining. This positive attitude to her illness is one of her greatest strengths. Combined with *yr*, this would give her tremendous resources to make a future for herself. Perhaps she should start to make women friends with whom she could relate in a less intense way.

Her next three runes are:

Rune 4 ᛒ *Beorc* in the centre of
           Being
Rune 5 ᛞ *Ger* hidden in the centre
           of *Being*
Rune 6 ᛋ *Sigil* in the realm of thought,
           the circle of *Thinking*.

Beorc is in the centre of her life. Since these close relationships are essential to her, yet the personnel change so regularly, maybe Margery is looking for a relationship rather than an individual with whom to be involved.

Ger, the treadmill rune, is hidden in the centre and may hold the key to the reason why she apparently keeps making the same mistakes. She said that from her Dad onwards she has always looked to men to care for her emotionally as well as physically, but has always ended up feeling smothered. Perhaps it would be a good time to change the pattern and perhaps do without a resident male for a while, relying on outside agencies to give her the support she needs with her disabilities.

Sigil, the sun or 'get up and go' rune is in her thoughts, suggesting, like *yr*, that it is her mind that will provide the key to her future as her body weakens, and that now is the time to learn the skills she will need to adapt to her worsening physical state. As *yr* shows, she does have the mental resources to perhaps take a training course that will give her a future career or even interests that do not rely on physical resources.

The last three runes are:

Rune 7 ᚩ *Os* hidden in the realm of everyday, the circle of *Doing*
Rune 8 ✕ *Nyd* hidden in *Is*
Rune 9 ⋈ *Man* in *Is*.

Os, the communication rune, is hidden in her realm of everyday existence, suggesting that she is not getting through to her partners what it is she really wants, not protection but acceptance of herself as still the attractive, intelligent person that she is. When they give her care and end up patronising her, she gets upset.

Nyd, also hidden in *Is*, is a not at all surprising rune to find with *os*. Her needs are hidden and very stuck, partly of course due to her disability which is getting worse. But also she hasn't really sorted out in her own mind what it is she really needs from her partners, and until she resolves this she can't even begin to communicate (*os*).

Rune 9, *man* in *Is*, provides the clue to the dilemma. When we get the 'strengths and weaknesses' rune stuck in *Is* it's a fair bet that the woman concerned is clinging on to the 'little girl lost' role emotionally, maybe because she is afraid that if she reveals her strengths she may end up alone.

Margery has been hiding her strengths for so many years she feels trapped. But it is only by revealing her strength of character and giving up the little girl role that she may find a relationship based on equality that will satisfy her needs, or else feel comfortable when she is alone.

It's easy to read the runes. What is not easy is facing head on those dilemmas that we hope will go away if we ignore them. You can't change the world but you can react to the problems positively and so at least write your own role in life's play.

Your cast of nine

Now try your first cast of nine, remembering to take three runes at a time, throw them, mark them on your chart at the back and see what they are suggesting before you add the next three. You may find these casts of nine useful about twice a week, but you can always use the casts of three or six when you are in a hurry or to answer a special question. Keep building up your rune of the day. If you wish, start to do this reading in the morning, to tune you into the current theme of the coming day.

ᚪ   *Ac* (*ark*) is the 'on the bike' or veto rune. If you get *ac* in a reading, then you've been pushed as far as you are prepared to go. If *ac* is hidden then you are feeling very threatened and helpless. Stand up for yourself – you've nothing to lose.

ᚫ   *Aesc* (*ask*) is the rune of stickability when the going gets rough. If you get *aesc* in a reading, then although life's a bit of a slog, it's telling you to stick at it a bit longer. If *aesc* is hidden, then you are running round in circles. Accept the situation and ask for help.

ᛦ   *Yr* (*year*) is the maturity or 'taking stock' rune. You know more than you think. In a reading it can indicate that your present situation may not be giving you scope to use all you know. Hidden, it is saying you may be operating at a redundant stage or level in your life. Time to move on.

Day 43

Iar
The beaver
– the rune
of
adaptability

Iar (pronounced *yar*) is the rune of the beaver (a bit of a pain with all those dams unless you're another beaver, but quite a slogger and amazingly adaptable to land or water). It is the rune of 'compromise' or 'meeting life half-way'. A woman's life is full of compromise. She does everything on the run and is incredibly adaptable at making the best out of any situation. Once she has accepted that the handsome prince got lost in the one-way system, she will use the pot at the end of the rainbow for cleaning up the cat sick or to catch the rain pouring through her bed-sit ceiling.

For if you can adapt to the way things are, then you can start moving forward. Adapt yourself to the reality of life at the wrong end of the rainbow and you can start to make things happen instead of watching the world go by. Of course it will be a bit of a slog – did you ever see a beaver in a deckchair? – but you'll find yourself doing all sorts of things you thought only other people were clever or young or beautiful or confident enough to do. Keep open-minded and adaptable and you are heading out of the muddy old creek for the open sea.

If you get *iar* in a reading, you know you are going to hit a hitch in your plans and will have to be prepared to do a patch job as usual. See how you can adapt the situation as it is, to get the most out of it.

If *iar* is hidden, then it is suggesting that

you are not using the situation to its best advantage. Don't waste time waiting for the ideal situation, time or person to turn up. They won't. Get on with life now.

Day 44

Ear
Dust – the rune of endings

Ear, (*ay-ar*) means dust and it is just that, the 'banging your head against a brick wall' rune. It is a gloomy old rune, telling us that in a particular situation (you'll know which one) you really are wasting your time.

Painful though it is to find out you're barking up the wrong tree, it can save a lot of wasted time and effort, and spare you a lot of heartache, if you accept that all your labours have turned to dust, and move on to pastures new. The relationship in which you've given your all just isn't going to work, or the job that was going to lead to a dazzling career has landed you in a back water with no chance of going forward. If we didn't have these cut-off points in our lives, we'd still be sitting in that oversized cradle chewing a rather dusty rusk.

Besides you can get a headache by banging that same old wall. Climb over it instead and see that on the other side is a whole new world, a blank slate for you to write on. For that's one thing we've learned as we've rattled our pebbles, that, at the end of the day, only we can be in that driving seat unless we really are prepared for others to dictate the route, the speed and the ultimate destination. But that's the joy of the busy woman's runes, no matter how far you have travelled on life's journey.

You don't have to change – you can still let other people dictate the moves. Only you'll accept that what is happening now is with your permission and knowledge so at least you can enjoy the ride.

Tomorrow brings the last rune, the most exciting of all. Have a peep over the wall – you might like the view.

If you get *ear* in a reading, then you are up against a situation that you know in your heart of hearts won't have a happy ending. Cut your losses now.

If *ear* is hidden, full marks for persistence. You keep on hoping beyond hope that it will turn out all right. Listen to yourself because deep down you do know you are kidding yourself on this one.

Day
45

Wyrd
The rune of fate, the destiny stone

We couldn't end on such a gloomy note as dust. For there is one rune left. The rune the Good Fairy used in Sleeping Beauty to make the Princess sleep for a hundred years instead of dying – the joker in the pack, the unknown element that makes life so exciting, and suddenly shakes the kaleidescope and changes the pattern of everything and opens a new road for you.

This rune is the blank – you don't have to draw anything at all on it, just leave both sides blank. This is the unknown quantity that whichever way it falls is giving no secrets away. It is sometimes called the stone of *Wyrd* (fate) or the Destiny Stone or the Stone of Wise Odin (remember the one hanging upside down on the tree who traded an eye for wisdom. But we are more interested in Mrs Odin gaining her wisdom on the run without the dramatics).

Are we saying that ultimately it is all up to some great force in the sky to determine our fortune? Quite the opposite. The stone is blank and only you can mark your destiny on it. Sometimes things don't go the way we had planned, though in many cases the way we act and what we are makes certain events or paths more likely to be open to us. Once we are aware of these patterns in ourselves, by using our runes to mirror these hidden aspects, then a lot of events we call chance do come under our control.

But what about the real unknowns, whether we call them the hand of fate, a deity's will or some random crashing of atoms? No one knows what causes these, though some will tell you they do, and so, no matter how you lock the doors of your house and your mind, you aren't 100 per cent safe from unexpected change. Frightening, of course but also very exciting. If every day was predictable then the human race would have died out with sheer boredom.

Though you can't control these unpredictable outside events, however they are caused, you can decide how you will react to them. At every point you can act or not act, accept or fight. Stay or leave. Only you can ultimately make those choices and you shouldn't let anyone else make them for you unless you have decided that is the way you want to run your life. Your runes can help you work your way through the possibilities and implications.

If you go to a clairvoyant she may well pick up from what you say the likely way your life might progress. Hey presto, she will prophesy a career change or a divorce and six months later it happens. Magic? Because of her you will, without realising it, start to make the prediction come true by behaving differently.

Psychologists call this the self-fulfilling prophecy. But why hand over your future for someone else to decide? Blanks are not something we are brought up to cope with. But empty spaces can be the best part of your life, especially if you are a busy woman. However much you fill your life with people or activity, you are always ultimately yourself and alone in the end.

The sooner you accept and welcome that, the sooner you'll stop collecting people and activities and shutting the curtains when it gets dark. Wasn't this where we started? Yes, only now the runes, not me are suggesting this might be true.

However little room you have to manoeuvre, there is always this one blank stone, the unknown quantity, this totally unpredictable move that makes you pull up your roots, kick over the traces and take the dangerous ride. It's the unknowable part of yourself that will only appear in a dire crisis when it's all or nothing. You go against everything you have been taught, think you believe and hold dear, and take a gamble.

Use your blank stone wisely and sparingly in your life. If you don't know what to do in a situation, don't act blindly or fall back on what you always do, don't ask your mother, your partner or your best friend.

Use your blank – draw breath, rev up for action and don't look down as you jump.

✳ *Iar(yar)* is the rune of compromise *Summary* and starting from where you are. If you get *iar* in a reading, then you'll find things aren't quite working out as you hoped and you'll need to make the best of a bad job. If *iar* is hidden then the ideal situation won't arise, so there is no point in waiting for that perfect tomorrow.

ᛠ *Ear* (*ay-ar*) is the rune of 'banging your head against a brick wall'. If you get *ear* in a reading, then you might as well accept you are wasting your time in a particular situation and cut your losses. If *ear* is hidden, then you haven't yet accepted that you're on a 'no through road'.

The Blank Stone – *Wyrd (weird)*, – your destiny to be filled in by you at regular intervals.

The final cast of nine before we go on our separate destinies.

Louisa's cast of nine

Louisa at 55 had been deserted by her husband for a younger woman after 30 years of marriage, leaving her completely alone.

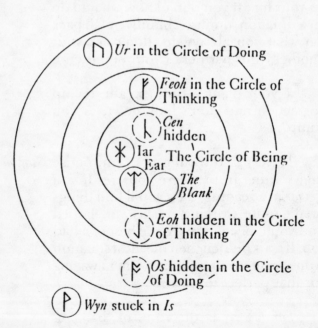

Ur in the Circle of Doing

Feoh in the Circle of Thinking

Cen hidden

Iar The Circle of Being
Ear

The Blank

Eoh hidden in the Circle of Thinking

Os hidden in the Circle of Doing

Wyn stuck in *Is*

From the verge of suicide, Louisa had pulled back with the help of good women friends though she was often lonely. Then she met Stephen who brought her flowers and chocolates and made her laugh. She made love for the first time since her husband had left and Stephen told her she was beautiful and desirable.

But as the months have passed, Stephen has made it clear he could never leave his wife, much as he loves Louisa. They are never able to go out together in the small town in which they live in case someone tells his wife 'which would break her heart'.

Louisa is torn by guilt and jealousy but she says surely what she has is better than nothing. It is a problem she thought only young women had and now finds herself cast into the role of the other women.

Louisa's reading

Rune 1 ᚳ *Cen,* the inner voice, is hidden in the centre of *Being*

Rune 2 ᚠ *Feoh,* the price, is in the realm of *thoughts*

Rune 3 ᚢ *Ur,* the obstacle rune, is in the circle of *Doing*

Rune 4 ᚩ *Os,* communication, is hidden in the circle of *Doing*

Rune 5 ᚹ *Wyn* is in *Is*

Rune 6 ᛇ *Eoh,* the realism rune, is hidden in the circle of *Thinking*

Rune 7 ᛡ *Iar,* the adaptable beaver, is in the circle of *Being*

Rune 8 ᛠ *Ear,* dust, banging your head against a brick wall, practically leapt out of the rune bag into the circle of *Being*

Rune 9 ○ The Blank, our personal good fairy, is next to dust, in the circle of *Being*.

You don't need me to tell you what the stones are saying any more. *Ear,* dust, is a dead giveaway, but at the end of the day only Louisa can decide that the relationship can't come to anything.

Feoh, the price in guilt and jealousy, is balanced by the pleasure she has from feeling she is a desirable woman again. But, of course, the hidden *os* suggests that someone isn't communicating the whole truth to all concerned. Any prizes for the name of Mr Have-it-all who isn't making any sacrifices, but is keeping his options well and truly open with his sweet words to both women?

Louisa does have the blank and the beaver of adaptability to help her if she decides to listen to what *eoh* the realistic rune is telling her: that she is going nowhere fast and needs to make a life for herself, perhaps by turning to her friends or finding a man who is free.

Wyn is the rune of joy, through herself not other people. She is holding back from making a life for herself by clinging on to the few crumbs of himself that Stephen can spare.

And that old inner voice *cen* is yelling away unheard in her centre, telling her the score and maybe reminding her how much she hated being the wronged wife. It's surprising how many strong women will act completely out of character when a man comes on the scene and starts whispering sweet nothings. Usually he manages to dodge the guilt.

Ur the obstacle of being alone and feeling unloved again is very much in her thoughts.

Making the decision to change isn't easy and sometimes you may need many, many readings to do what you know is the best course. Sometimes even then you won't feel ready to leap. Remember to be kind to yourself, your own best friend. Forgive yourself your weaknesses and failures and go forward.

Interpreting the runes

Keep faith with yourself as you struggle home with your umpteen bags of shopping to the mountain of unwashed dishes and brain-dead teenagers. Don't lose heart as you open the door of your bedsit and think 'Is this what the golden freedom I dreamed of is all about?' Hang on as you watch your retirement cruise, planned to be taken once the kids were off your hands, sail without you because your old mother can't be left alone. But, whatever your problems, remember that the runes are telling you that *you* are special, *you* are magic and when you doubt it take out your stones and feel the power within and from yourself. So go out there and confront those obstacles and say, 'I will be happy no matter what spanners life throws in the works'.

It is that wonderful, exciting unpredictable future before you, the fortune that you are still to make. Even if you are 90 there are still new mountains to climb though you may be slower and need more rests on the way up. One person I know began a career as a commercial artist at the age of 80 having decided to stop practising and get on with the real thing. Look in the mirror and be glad the person you see is you. I hope the book has helped you to find your own way. Once you have learned the runes and how to interpret them, adapt the method to suit your needs and develop your own way of talking with your runes. In a few months you will look back at your early readings as you would read an old diary and be amazed how far you have travelled.

THE RUNES

Symbol, name, pronunciation and meaning

Feoh (fay-oh) is the price you must pay for achieving what you want or for maintaining the *status quo*. If hidden, the price is more than it seems.

Ur (err) shows the obstacle blocking your ambitions. If hidden, it may be telling you that you need the obstacle and don't want change.

Thorn (thorn) reveals the petty annoyances building up. If it is hidden, then perhaps you feel you've no right to get cross with those who are annoying you.

Os (oas) shows something important has to be said. If *os* is hidden you may be listening to yesterday's conversation.

Rad (rard) suggests change is long overdue which may be hard but promises excitement. If *rad* is hidden, are you taking the soft option while complaining you don't like the way things are?

Cen (ken), your inner voice, is rarely wrong. It may mean you have been receiving a lot of conflicting advice. If *cen* is hidden you may be letting other people dictate your destiny.

Gyfu (geefoo), rune of giving, can indicate you are being asked to give too much. If *gyfu* is hidden, then maybe you are giving out of unnecessary guilt and should give to yourself more.

Wyn (win), rune of joy and separateness, may indicate that other people can't bring you total happiness. If *wyn* is hidden, perhaps you are afraid of being alone and abandoned.

Haegel (hargool), the rune of hassle, may show you are caught in the crossfire of someone else's running battle. If *haegel* is hidden then perhaps you are too afraid of upsetting people by saying no, although perhaps you should.

Nyd (need), rune of needs, can indicate that your own needs are important and perhaps aren't being met. Hidden, *nyd* may suggest you are denying these needs through guilt.

Is (eess) rune of ice, can indicate those circumstances stopping you progressing. Hidden, it can indicate you are freezing yourself in a situation through fear of change.

Ger (gair), rune of the seasons, can indicate a time of natural change. *Ger* hidden, may mean you are stuck in the old patterns and making the same mistakes.

Eoh (yo), the 'limitations' rune, can indicate disappointments but can also help clear the ground to go forward. *Eoh* hidden may show your expectations are unrealistic.

Peorth (pay-orth), the grassroots rune, can uncover someone who's been trying to blind you with science. *Peorth* hidden may suggest that you have accepted other people pulling your strings.

Eohl (yole) is the magic 'you' that 'knows' what is going to happen, not through logic but inspiration. *Eohl* hidden means you've been relying on others for the magic answer.

Sigil (seegle) the 'go for it' rune, can indicate the time is right for change. If *sigil* is hidden, then you are probably feeling frustrated at just being the spectator.

Tir (tear), the sacrifice rune, can suggest the right time to shed comfortable old ways that keep you safe but bored. If it is hidden, you may be making the wrong sacrifices.

Beorc (bay-ork), rune of close relationships, may be telling you to sort out old family rivalries. If *beorc* is hidden, then you are trapped in the old games and need to see yourself as a person in your own right.

Eh (em), rune of harmony and balance, may be telling you to take time out to regain your equilibrium. If *eh* is hidden, then your attempts to be a peacemaker may be inadvertently fuelling disharmony around you.

Man (man), rune of strengths and weaknesses, can tell you to blow your own trumpet. If it is hidden, then you could be playing down your own abilities in order to make others feel good.

Lagu (largoo), is the rune which can tell you to trust your feelings. If it is hidden then perhaps you are trying to be too calm and controlled.

Ing (ing), rune of withdrawal, may be telling you to walk away from whatever is hurting you. Hidden, it may indicate that you are lashing out at everyone but only hurting yourself.

Odal (owed-al) deals with practical issues. It may indicate that these issues are blocking progress so sort them out. Hidden, it can mean you are doing more than your fair share of the dirty work but don't like to protest.

Daeg (darg) can indicate that you are on the right path at last. If *daeg* is hidden then the answer is there, very close to home.

Ac (ark), rune of independence, can show you have been pushed as far as you are prepared to go. If *ac* is hidden you may be feeling threatened and helpless, so it is time to stand up for yourself.

Aesc (ask) rune of endurance, can tell you to keep slogging. If *aesc* is hidden, then you are running round in circles. Accept the situation and ask for help.

Yr (year) can indicate that your situation may not be giving you scope to use all you know. Hidden, it is saying you may be at a redundant stage and it is time to move on.

Iar (yar), the adapatability rune, can show that maybe you have hit a problem and need to adapt your plans. If *iar* is hidden, perhaps you're burying your head in the sand.

Ear (ay-ar) is the rune of dust. It can show that it's time to call it a day in a particular situation. If *ear* is hidden, perhaps you're burying your head in the sand.

The Blank Stone. *Wyrd (weird),* your destiny to be filled in by you at regular intervals.

The central circle of *Being* talks about the real you. Runes falling here touch on pretty important issues. If the rune is hidden or the circle empty, perhaps you are a bit out of touch with what matters to you. *The casting cloth*

   Runes that fall into the circle of *Thinking,* stand for issues very much on your mind. If they are hidden, you may be living too much in your head and not translating the plans into action.

Runes in the circle of *Doing,* tend to deal with your everyday preoccupations. Hidden, they show crossed wires or criticism.

Runes in *Is,* the area outside the circles, mean you are stuck. If hidden, then you may be obstructing yourself.

Hidden runes can show that you are not facing the issue. Clusters (groups of runes) are stones that fall together and deal with the same issue.

Runes covering each other indicate that one is dominating or distorting another.

Rune Chart 1

Rune of the Day

Day	Symbol	Name	Meaning
1			
2			
3			
4			
5			
6			
7			
8			
9			
10			
11			
12			
13			
14			
15			
16			
17			
18			
19			
20			
21			

Day	Symbol	Name	Meaning
22			
23			
24			
25			
26			
27			
28			
29			
30			
31			
32			
33			
34			
35			
36			
37			
38			
39			
40			
41			
42			

Now you may wish to keep your own rune diary of the rune of the day. You may find that your rune meaning changes as you make the system your own.

Recording your Casts of Three

Ideally, if you have the time and patience the best way to record your rune casts is to draw three circles like the diagrams I have used in this book and mark on them exactly how the runes fall — circling and shading those that are hidden.

But the busy woman will probably find it easier to use this chart. Simply enter the date and draw the runes in the appropriate box — putting them in a circle if they are hidden. Here's how our first Cast of Three — Ellie's — would have looked under this system.

DATE	BEING	THINKING	DOING	IS
		Ⓡ	ᚠ	ᚦ

DATE	BEING	THINKING	DOING	IS

Recording your Casts of Six

This is no more difficult than the cast of three — we just use slightly bigger boxes.

DATE	BEING	THINKING	DOING	IS

Recording your Casts of Nine

The boxes get even bigger — but the system is still as simple.

DATE	BEING	THINKING	DOING	IS

Opening
doors to
the World
of books

BOOK TOKEN

Book Tokens

Book Tokens
can be
bought and
exchanged
at most
bookshops